Quotes of the Year 2009
He Said ... She Said

Bernard Share

Gill & Macmillan

Gill & Macmillan Ltd
Hume Avenue, Park West, Dublin 12
with associated companies throughout the world
www.gillmacmillan.ie

978 07171 4600 0

Index compiled by Cover to Cover
Typography design by Make Communication
Print origination by Carole Lynch
Printed in the UK by CPI Cox and Wyman

This book is typeset in Linotype Minion and
Neue Helvetica.

The paper used in this book comes from the wood pulp of
managed forests. For every tree felled, at least one tree is
planted, thereby renewing natural resources.

5 4 3 2 1

Contents

Preface

I was once a partner in a design consultancy we called Verbiage, for no better reason than that we offered words (me) as well as graphics (him). Since those heady days, the word has on many occasions come back to haunt me in various guises, and never more so than in the confection of this present undertaking. Listen to any one hour of any radio chat show, for example, and you will conclude that the task is impossible: as a nation we consume words at an unconscionable rate—if they left a carbon footprint, this island would lead the world in verbal pollution.

But just listen—to the chat show, the pub talk, the oul' wan next door—and even from the lips of those, and there are many, who talk faster than they think, there falls the occasional bon mot like manna from heaven, or the equivalent from the other place. We do, uncontrovertibly, have the gift of the gab, or to put it more pertinently perhaps, the innate ability to shape a phrase around experience, to distil a verbal essence from something only half-apprehended. When Oscar Wilde confessed 'I wish I had said that', he was revealing his nationality as much as his capacity for envy.

Thus the selection of these 1,600-odd Quotes of the Year has been concerned very nearly as much with form as with content—the artfully expressed banality earns its place beside the considered phrasing of the politician, the innocent inwardness of the nerd and the anorak. One must also seek, if not always find, the added ingredient which will keep the original utterance fresh long enough for it to remain palatable in these pages. This, of course, does not always work: something that seemed munificently meaningful in March can become a tattered nothing by November. I would hope, of course, that such instances have remained very much in the minority; but time and personal taste will make their own selection.

What follows, it must be emphasised, in no way sets out to be a history in soundbites of the passing year: such chronicles are readily available elsewhere and it is not always the events that shake the nation that are productive of the most enduring apothegms. No: what he said/she said during the months that are past is just that: a mirror to our manners, manoeuvrings and meanderings which, I would hope, reflects something of the character of this particular part of what we are.

Bernard Share
October 2009

September 2008

It's good to be back!

Thus Brian Dooher, victorious Tyrone captain, accepting the County's third Sam Maguire in a decade. But for the political classes returning from their modest vacations, the feeling is not quite as euphoric. With the world economy apparently on the road to ruin, September holds little to be cheerful about unless you are a Tyrone supporter or a Kilkenny Cat. No more Celtic Tiger, hope sinking with the Asgard ii, *and Signor Trapattoni struggling to manage our second national language. The coolest September since 1994. Cliché of the Month: 'going forward'.*

PARTY LINES

I can see no reason, politically, legally, morally, why the Executive should not be sitting. *Peter Robinson, Northern Ireland First Minister.*

Under par

In the time the Government have been away on holidays, their July predictions for the economy have been shown to be 100 per cent off-target. It is now time that the Government put away their golf clubs, suntan lotion and Dan Brown paperbacks and got a grip on the deteriorating Irish economy. *Fine Gael financial spokesman Richard Bruton.*

Knowing the score

So, why are you losers? Because losers you are. *Rugby commentator George Hook berates a Fine Gael think-in gathering.*

Policy platform

If you ask me on a wet Monday morning whose side I am on—the commuter who's standing at the railway station waiting for a train that isn't coming because somebody took an official strike—I have no hesitation in saying I'm on the side of the working person who's being delayed in getting to work. *Labour Party leader Eamon Gilmore.*

Counter attack

I did not punch him. I have never punched anybody in a pub in my life. I certainly didn't catch him by the throat with my left hand, my right hand or any other hand . . . I have never grabbed anybody by the throat in a pub in my life. *Minister for Defence Willie O'Dea, accused of attacking a man in a Limerick pub. The allegation was dismissed and the accuser sentenced to a jail term.*

Mad Hatter's PD party

I don't want to have my head buried in the sand or live in an Alice in Wonderland kind of environment. *Minister for Health & Children and former PD leader Mary Harney contemplates the predicted demise of her party.*

Regressive Democrats

We had to dispel that uncertainty and the parliamentary party had a very frank meeting of all four members, and the collective opinion was that the party is no longer politically viable. *Party leader Senator Ciaran Cannon.*

Here's your hat and what's your hurry?

Is there an opportunity to give them three to six months of benefit? Foreign workers in Ireland could be given a lump sum payment of up to six months' worth of unemployment if they agree to return home. *Fine Gael TD Leo Varadkar.*

I love this country. People are very wonderful, happy and accommodating. It could happen anywhere. *Nigerian actor Uche Odikanwa following an attack on him in Dublin.*

Fowl play

Featherless but still plump State hens. *Civil servants as perceived by Minister of State John McGuinness.*

Ten civil servants [in his private and ministerial offices] makes the Minister of State Deputy John McGuinness a pretty plump State gander. *Labour leader Eamon Gilmore.*

Contempt of court

I was a conveyancing solicitor and as I understand it a lot of them are being laid off at the moment—but then people don't really care about lawyers. *Arlene Foster, Northern Ireland Minister for Enterprise, Trade & Employment.*

Man to Mahon

A lot of issues raised here were always picked out to try and trap me and trick me. I never in public life took a bribe, backhander or anything else . . . I did my best in front of this tribunal to tell the truth. *Final statement of Bertie Ahern to the Mahon Tribunal.*

ONLY A GAME

You say to me that there is more to life than hurling. Well if you want to carry on like a fella who is not an intercounty hurler, well then there will be more to life than hurling. Lots more. But there won't be hurling. That's the reality of it. *Kilkenny manager Brian Cody.*

Shutting his trap

I am a Trappist. I am a Trappist. I don't speak but I think a great deal. *National coach Giovanni Trapattoni on the eve of the first World Cup match.*

What's his knowledge of the Irish players? How well does he know how the Irish players feel and what they are all about? Because I think we are a little bit different. *Former coach Steve Staunton on his successor.*

Flushed with success

But this year there was only one candidate. As inhabitants of a smaller city, Dublin's poker players are a more close-knit bunch and have a reputation for being friendlier and more laid-back than London's. A worthy winner. *Philip Conneller, editor of* Bluff Europe, *on Dublin being named the best poker-playing city in Europe.*

Hither and sliotar

We adhere to all the rules and regulations of the GAA. You shouldn't be asking me that question because that would be breaking the rules and we adhere to them. *Gaelic Gear manager Fintan O'Hagan, asked whether or not his company imported sliotars.*

Polished delivery

This cup has been partying hard for years now and there were a lot of dents, knocks and bruises on it. We even had to rub off the name of a fan who managed to scrape his signature onto the bottom of it. It definitely needed a good bit of TLC. *James Mary Kelly, Kilkenny, on the refurbishment of the replica of the Liam McCarthy trophy, for which he was originally responsible.*

It didn't

It will be a wonderful day for Waterford, especially for younger people who never knew the euphoria of 1948 and 1959. Those were magical days for us. The aftermath of the '48 victory on The Quay was unbelievable and I honestly believe it is going to happen again. *Larry Fanning, member of the 1948 Waterford team, who died a week before the 2008 final.*

Impact statement

I never got hit by a car or anything, like, but it certainly feels as close as you could get to it. *Waterford manager Davy Fitzgerald on losing the hurling final to Kilkenny.*

Ring fencing

The man is a clown. The word 'clown' just suits him. You've been to the circus, you've laughed at clowns. They're not doing anything, but you laugh at them—I'm laughing at him. *Former Republic of Ireland captain and Sunderland manager Roy Keane disapproves of FIFA Vice-President Jack Warner.*

Aristocats

You dream of an ideal performance but it never happens. You dream of winning every ball and every contest when you are in a final but it never turns out like that. Except last week for Kilkenny. *Cork hurling star Seán Óg Ó hAilpín.*

The horse's mouth

Ireland has now got a nasty thing about doping of human beings and animals . . . internationally we are now a joke. *Pat Hickey, president of the Olympic Council of Ireland.*

THAT SINKING FEELING

We were about 12 miles to the west of the island of Belle-Île, in a southwesterly wind of force five to six, good sea conditions. We had a very fast ingress of water into the hull. We were unable to trace its source. I had to make the decision to abandon ship. *Colm Newport, captain of the sail-training brigantine* Asgard ii.

Order to view

I've always wanted to see the inside of a lifeboat and now I finally have. And we have the captain to thank for that—to get us off the boat in five minutes was absolutely brilliant. Asgard ii *crew member Holly Byrne.*

Hail and farewell

I was on the ship's first sailing, and my daughter was on the last—I launched it and she sank it. *Pioneer crew member Jean Campbell.*

CALLS OF NATURE

If there is an eel or a frog or a particular kind of animal in Ireland, the actual animal which gives it that definition is kept in the National Museum. That eel might have been caught in Co. Mayo in the 1770s and we still have that in a tub. There are fish in that tank that saw Parnell! *Pat Wallace, Director of the National Museum of Ireland.*

Fur and feather

The parrots screech in the bedroom next to ours and we would like the parrots to be moved. We live in a semi-detached house. We tried to speak reasonably to the neighbour but we have received verbal abuse and threatening abuse. There are four dogs living in that house since 2005. The dogs were living in the bedroom so we complained but nothing happened and we were told what we could do with ourselves. Since 2007 the two dogs in the bedroom have been replaced by two parrots. *Julie Morris, Newbridge, Co. Kildare.*

Blind side

Men see going to the doctor as a weakness. You are a weak man and you are fragile, but it is the opposite. I think it is much better to have the courage to say that you went to the doctor than actually leaving it to Mother Nature to cure you and find out that it is too late. *Leinster and Argentine fly-half Dr Felipe Contepomi.*

Rhubarb rhubarb

The giant rhubarb or *gunnera* is now a major problem in the west of Ireland and has invaded Achill. Bringing in alien species is a little like minding mice at the crossroads; you never know what will take off. *Peter Wyse Jackson, Director, National Botanic Gardens.*

Champignons League

I saw the players eating mushrooms before a friendly. I was stunned into silence for several seconds. *Giovanni Trapattoni disapproves of pre-match feasting on fungus.*

Whale of a time

We've waited a long time, for some of us a lifetime, but we are delighted to announce that blue whales have been observed and photographed in southwest waters. *Pádraig Whooley, sightings co-ordinator for the Irish Whale and Dolphin Group.*

Frontal attack

If you could organise a female next year I'd be extremely grateful. *Michael O'Leary, Ryanair chief executive, thanks a half-naked environmental protestor for his contribution to the company's AGM.*

How's Triggs?

There's me, Triggs, and I've got a new German shepherd. I'm taking the lead role, as you'd expect you've got to take the lead role, and the German shepherd has taken over and he's second in charge. Poor old Triggs is at the back. *Sunderland soccer manager Roy Keane, dogged by his need to run the show.*

Won by a whisker

Sure, we'd a meeting one night and one of us asked, 'What can we do different this year?' and I answered, 'Grow beards'. I just thought it would be a bit of craic. *Ryan McMenamin, corner/wing back on the winning Tyrone team.*

Pollan count

We are already trying very hard to save endangered fish species in Lough Derg such as pollan and gilaroo trout. Extracting such a huge volume of water from the lake could finally wipe out these species forever and threaten spawning conditions for trout and salmon in local rivers if waters went very low. *Kevin Grimes, chairman of the Lough Derg Anglers' Association, on the threat to pipe Shannon water to Dublin.*

ARTS AND PARTS
It's like childbirth. We stop doing it long enough to forget how painful it is. And then we do it all over again. It's ridiculous. For 20 years I've been saying I'm never doing that again, and then I do because it's a brilliant piece. Therein lies all human life in its nakedness and foolishness and honesty . . . It's the most painful thing I've ever done on stage in my life. I've never used so much energy doing nothing. *Stephen Brennan on playing Lucky in Beckett's* Waiting for Godot.

Talespin
I always try to have a twist in the tale, which I feel is one of the reasons for my success. I try very hard to be unpredictable. Why is chick lit so successful at the moment? I think it's because people want to read about their own lives, especially women. That's the only reason I can think of. *Melissa Hill, launching her seventh novel.*

Fare City
The public could end up too scared to get into a cab because our drivers are being portrayed so badly in *Fair City*. They're shown as callous murderers who lock people up in the boot of their cars and then go out the next day as if nothing happened. It's a despicable way of portraying the hard-working taxi drivers in this country. *Tommy Gorman, president, National Taxi Drivers' Union.*

Clefhanger
One of the conclusions I've come to is that choral music and choral concerts need to tell a story. Because, after all, the one thing that singers have that instrumentalists don't is the text. Therefore, the crucial point is, surely, what the hell are they singing about? *Paul Hillier, Director of the National Chamber Choir.*

Empty gesture
I must admit I do find it comical RTÉ using Dad's chair in their promos. We sometimes joke that a better memorial would have been

two fingers pointing to Donnybrook and Leinster House. Not only did RTÉ disappoint Dad continually by scrapping his shows, they only started showing *Father Ted* because they were losing ratings to Channel 4. *Dermot Morgan's son Don.*

Star turn

It became a whimsy of mine to finish the story, just for my own peace of mind. I often wondered how Douglas Adams would have resurrected his beloved characters. And now, almost a quarter of a century after reading *Hitchhiker*, I have been given the incredible opportunity of writing the next chapter in the saga myself. *Wexford children's writer Eoin Colfer.*

Such is life

I was really, really lonely. I mean it is so far away, and it was a weird job. I was on what's known as weather cover, where you're on standby in case it rains, and if it does they will shoot your scene. It was Australia so it never did. There was loads of hanging around and loads of time to think and get depressed, and I did. I mean I was still just a teenager. It was really hard. *Actress Kerry Condon on shooting* Ned Kelly, *her first major film.*

The lady vanishes

A large proportion of art students are women. Then most of them just disappear. Arrogance is a large part of success for an artist here. *Rita Duffy, President, Royal Ulster Academy of Arts.*

Out of keys

The truth is that we've been putting on concerts since 1995, but we've never owned a piano. So every time our group, Music for New Ross, wanted to have a pianist, we had to hire an instrument. In 2005 the husband of one of our committee members said, 'Well, next time you're getting a piano, why don't you do more than one concert?' Almost immediately the idea exploded. So we're doing a piano festival because we don't have a piano. Which is quite sensible, when you think about it. *Connie Tantrum, festival director.*

Filthy lucre

We just want to make as much money as possible. We know dirt sells. We want to position Ireland to the world as a place where the celebrities are and where you should be too. *Ray Senior, owner of photo agency VIP Ireland.*

Better than one?

They tend to show a lot of 'shock docs' after nine o'clock about a man with two heads. I hope that's not the future of television. *Dermot Horan, director of broadcasting acquisitions, RTÉ, on rival TV3's prime-time slot.*

Hé hé hé

Roddy's work is full of that life force, and the French recognise that in stuff like *The Commitments*, and they adore it because they see people who are beaten down all the time and hop up like nothing happened and make fun of themselves, and there is maybe something Gallic in all of that. *Actress Olwen Fouéré, playing in Paris in a French language version of* Paula Spencer—The Woman who Walked into Doors.

Head start

There's a statistic which says that 70 per cent of actors are the youngest in their family, and there's another statistic even stranger— 40 per cent of actors have a parent in the mental-health industry. My mother's a psychotherapist, so I'm just a fecking cliché. *Roscommon actor Chris O'Dowd.*

On song

The most important thing for me, to be able to make a painting, is music. If I haven't got the right songs, I can't do it. I'm trying, on a canvas, to make somebody feel the way I feel when I hear the music. *Donegal artist Marty Kelly.*

Happy medium

One thing my mother always told me is never lose the run of yourself, you're never as good as the papers say you are and never as bad as the papers say you are. *RTÉ 'Liveline' presenter Joe Duffy.*

Rock in the cradle

I must say Bono, as he called himself, had a lovely voice. Joyful and charming. I remember it ringing out around the room as he went through his scales. After he finished I complimented him on his range and performance. *Singing coach Veronica Dunne recalling how rock 'n' roll's gain was opera's loss.*

In memoriam

It's just so much part of Dublin and I'm a real Dubliner. I've a huge feeling for this wonderful old theatre. *Mezzo-soprano Bernadette Greevy, leaving a brass imprint of her hands outside the Gaiety Theatre. Dr Greevy died on 26 September.*

We were privileged to know her and even more privileged to hear her. She decorated our lives with her rare jewel of a voice and continued to contribute to our cultural life through her wonderful Anna Livia Opera Festival. *Minister for Arts Martin Cullen, on Bernadette Greevy.*

MAMMON

I don't take holidays. What would people do without De Paper? *James Buckley, 54 years a* Cork Examiner/Examiner/Irish Examiner *delivery boy.*

The penny drops

The definition of a recession is if you have two consecutive quarters of contracting economic activity. The cso has confirmed that that is the case, and whilst unwelcome, that is the case. *Taoiseach Brian Cowen.*

Well, there you are now. Cowenomics seems to be a brand all of its own. It just got slumpier and slumpier and by the end of the year it might be even worse. *Labour finance spokeswoman Joan Burton.*

Human touch

All sorts of autonomous behaviour is happening, even on the web. Microsoft xp and Vista, for example, carry out updates themselves. They are still at the point, however, where human intervention happens at certain times. *Paddy Nixon, sfi professor of distributed systems, ucd.*

Homes sweet homes

I need to earn my wages because I have a lot of properties, none of which I rent. I have two in England and five in Ireland so it's sort of crazy. I love doing up property and that's tended to be where I put my money. But, of course, I find these wonderful places and can't bear to part with them. *Actor Jeremy Irons.*

Accounts rendered

This is a terrible invasion of privacy and could well lead to farmers being the target of criminal gangs in search of easy pickings. I have been contacted by many people who are very distressed and upset by this outlandish regulation. They believe there is nothing left now but to open up their bank accounts and tell people to go into the bank and ask for their details. *Michael Ring TD on an EU regulation under which the names of farmers, their address (county and town) and details of the amount received by them would be published on the Department website.*

I would worry. Is there a slightly more sinister underlying reason for publishing the payments to discredit the system so [they] can cut it in time? *MEP Mairéad McGuinness.*

Bank checks

The state guarantee is provided at a price. It is not for free. The state guarantee will have a mechanism whereby a fee reflecting commercial realities will have to be paid by those banks which may access the liquidity provided by the Central Bank. *Taoiseach Brian Cowen.*

I can see what is in it for the six bank chief executives, who between themselves earn €13m a year. I cannot see what is in it for the people or the taxpayers who may yet foot the bill. *Labour leader Eamon Gilmore.*

Sore thing

Like a massive bent erection. *Paul Walsh, chairman of the Pembroke Road Residents' Association, on the plan for a 57-storey tower at Ballsbridge, Dublin.*

LIQUID ASSETS

Appalling and totally unacceptable. *Galway mayor Pádraig Conneely on learning that both the normal and emergency water supplies of the city are lead-contaminated.*

Most of the people in Mervue are back to buying bottled water and won't touch anything else. We've become like Spain. *Galway Progressive Democrat councillor Terry O'Flaherty.*

Small ones

Put it this way, we will not need a lorry to ferry away what we have seized. *Donegal Garda spokesperson on liquor confiscated from people drinking in public places.*

Home brew

This site announcement is a truly significant decision by Diageo. Not only are we demonstrating our commitment to Ireland, we are also staying true to the roots and heritage of the Guinness brand and Arthur himself. *Brian Duffy, Guinness Global Brand Director, on the decision to build a new brewery on Guinness land at Leixlip, Co. Kildare.*

Fast forward

If people want to go out for a meal on Good Friday I would have thought they could have a drink with their meal. Technically you [the Garda inspector] are correct, but I think myself it is absolutely ludicrous that people on holidays especially cannot have a glass of wine with their meal. *Judge Mary Fahy marks the facts proven but records no convictions in prosecutions involving several publicans.*

Pint taken

It's misleading to call me an heiress. I can understand why people do, because of the name and all that, but the way I look at it is that I've got four grandparents. One of them is Desmond; he's Anglo-Irish and his name is Guinness. It's a very small bit of who I am. *Supermodel Jasmine Guinness.*

Way out

[It] causes incredible traffic noise and congestion with a cacophony of cars' horns screeching, cat-calling, doors banging, screaming and singing as patrons wend their way across the road. Sometimes, there can be a shortage of taxis or people linger during summertime or else set off up the Howth Road or along the Crescent, urinating, vomiting, overturning bins, fighting, breaking wing mirrors, singing and shouting as they go. *Local resident Stephen Moran on the exodus of young drinkers from a Fairview, Dublin leisure centre in the small hours.*

Jarring note
There were no drug dealers at the table when the social partners were discussing how to tackle the problem of drug abuse. So why are the alcohol industry at the table? They will do anything to protect their profits. Meanwhile, hundreds of lives are being lost. *Dr Bobby Smyth, Irish College of Psychiatrists.*

HOME AND AWAY
He is a dictator. He tries to control everything. I don't want him to control Ireland. *French waiter Michael Audren, Drumshanbo, charged with attempting to throw eggs at President Nicolas Sarkozy during his Dublin visit.*

Both your houses
How dare he castigate our city like that? I'm sure Councillor Mulcahy knows that there are some pretty nasty people in Clare. What he said is downright stupid. *Limerick mayor John Gilligan denies a claim that if the proposal to relocate Limerick people were implemented, Shannon and Co. Clare would end up with the 'dregs of society'.*

Youthful attraction
Since he was four years old, steam-powered machines have always held a fascination for Seán as we had to get specially adapted pedals to drive his grandfather's traction engine. *Mary Quigg, Mountcharles, Co. Donegal, on her eleven-year-old son becoming the first Irish person to win the overall Steam Apprentice Award at the World Steam Rally in Dorset, UK.*

Tanks a million
It was very hard to wrap. So I just stuck a Christmas tree on top of it. *Eileen Curtis, The Curragh, Co. Kildare, on buying her husband a 63-tonne Chieftain tank for Christmas.*

Ruling Britannia

We were honoured that Nakheel came to an Irish person to buy the island of England. There was lots of talk about Richard Branson and Rod Stewart wanting to buy it and there are some very annoyed people in England who thought they had it but didn't get it. *Property magnate John Dolan on acquiring the island in 'The World' development in Dubai.*

Entente cordiale

In retrospect, it can be said that de Gaulle did us a good turn in blocking our entry until we were much better prepared for membership. *T.K. Whitaker, author of the seminal 1958 'First Programme for Economic Expansion', on Ireland's failed application to join the European Economic Community in 1961.*

Vicious circle

A lot of foreign buses using 'sat navs' are entering the Ring of Kerry the wrong way round and getting stuck in the tunnel. *Tom Doherty, Killarney County Councillor.*

What is my nation?

There is, of course, nothing wrong with being a British national. The point can fairly be made, however, that it is not on that Mr Ganley, who now wishes to proclaim himself as an Irish businessman, should choose to describe himself as British on UK company returns over a number of years. *Minister of State Dick Roche castigates Libertas founder Declan Ganley.*

Stamp of approval

I think postcodes are like brands. It is similar to driving a BMW or wearing a Cartier watch. Many buyers from outside Dublin or non-nationals have bought into the Dublin 4 factor and aspire to that status. I have met non-Irish who are in Ireland maybe only 48 hours and will only rent in Dublin 4. *Owen Reilly of Owen Reilly New Homes.*

Abroad band

This is a graduation ceremony which befits the times, being green, time-efficient and involving a low carbon footprint. *Niall McEvoy, industrial liaison manager, IT Sligo, on Ireland's first virtual conferring ceremony involving graduates in eight countries.*

Fáilte isteach

I dread getting off the plane, then that walk to the desk. Now my husband accompanies me, no matter how long the queue is, in the non-EU line. He stands next to me, because I always feel I'm going to get harassed. I get in knots every time I go through. *Malaysian-born Dr Angie Chong, 25 years an Irish resident, on the immigration regime at Dublin airport.*

Celtic highlight

There are so many things I love about Ireland. The tweed. The linen. The houses. The perfection. Even the mingy little cottages are beautiful. *Shoe designer Manolo Blahnik.*

FAITH AND MORALS

It is better together. This is one of the lessons I bring from the segregated city of Belfast where churches in violent black spots are making a real difference by working together across the sectarian divide. *Bishop Trevor Williams, former BBC reporter in Northern Ireland, at his installation in Limerick cathedral.*

Tea and empathy

It was while she was here having a cup of tea that she said that she would like to come back to us and this is where she would like to come for a retreat. Every year she comes here and her husband, Martin, jokes that it is a break for him and he can go off and play golf. *Sr Bernardine, Abbess of the Poor Clares' monastery in Ennis, on a visit by President Mary McAleese in 1997.*

All things to all men

It will be multi-faith religious education instead of a Catholic programme. It will be one common programme initially and we will address the main tenets of faith, the commonalities shared by faiths, rather than separating them into different religions. *David Campbell, Principal, Scoil Ghráinne, Phibblestown, Co. Meath, Ireland's first Community-style primary school.*

It was a pretty radical Protestant sect, but nowadays we like to think of ourselves as neither Protestant nor Catholic. Belief is not that important to us. We see ourselves as seekers rather than ones who find the one unalloyed truth. *Rev. Bill Darlison, minister at Dublin's Unitarian church.*

Model answer

Ireland is still full of religious prudes and an anti-female attitude, something which the Church has a lot to answer for. *Model Claire Tully addressing students at University College Dublin.*

MIND YOUR LANGUAGE

This is my fourth season in Paris. I arrived over in July 2005 with school French. The language is fine now but initially it was the most difficult thing. It's not a barrier any more. *Mick Carroll, Racing Club de Paris rugby player.*

Lost for words

We joined because the Irish Army weren't recruiting at the time. Me and Molly [Ian Malone] had two choices: either the British Army or the French Foreign Legion. And neither of us could speak French, so that was that. *Dubliner and British Army sergeant Gavin O'Neill.*

A matter of forms

In this country, citizens provide votes at election time and then find that those they have elected are totally controlled by rules, regulations, plans, protocols, directives, agreements, strategies, guidelines and interpretations. *Mayo County Councillor Paddy McGuinness.*

Mobile top-up

In many other European countries, things that can't move are taxed more than things that can move, that are mobile, and can move from one part of the world to the other. *Minister for Health & Children Mary Harney.*

Naysayer

There are known knowns. These are the things we know we know. We also know there are known unknowns. That is to say we know there are some things that we do not know. There are also unknown unknowns, the ones we don't know we don't know. *Nicholas Bond, director of environmental and emergency services at Cork County Council, addressing the annual environment conference on the subject of illegal dumping in Co. Cork.*

I'm not worried at all

says Louis Walsh, music impresario, of the looming recession: 'I don't need materialistic things because I have enough of them—people in my industry are overpaid anyway. Money has brought too much fake tan, fake hair and fake tits to Ireland.' As the crisis deepens, banks are bailed out, ill-conceived budget measures excoriated: the grey wing turns the tide. Ireland wins in Australia. Cliché of the Month: 'deleveraging'.

Mammy! Mammy!
People cannot internalise the magnitude of this crisis, which will metastasise into the mother of all recessions. *Ray Kinsella, professor of banking and financial services, UCD.*

No Harvey no
In 50 years of involvement in the industry I have never seen such disappointing sales as there were in Ireland at the end of the 2007/08 financial year. *Gerry Harvey, the loud voice of Australian retailer Harvey Norman.*

Auto suggestion
If you see a whole load of airlines going out of business, routes being cut, tourism falling off, companies going bust, but the M50 is still chock-a-block with cars, the message I take from that is that cars is where you need to be concentrating. I don't see too much evidence yet of people abandoning their cars. *Geoffrey O'Byrne White, CEO, CityJet, on rising oil prices.*

Going with the flow
Nothing that anyone does now on a regulatory level will turn the turmoil taps off. There is no magic bullet solution or it would have come many months ago. *EU Commissioner Charlie McCreevy.*

Tragically, Breakfast Roll Man has been struggling to hold on to his job since last September. *Former government minister and turf accountant Ivan Yates.*

You know that from a political point of view I would have managed the challenge. But, as we know, that's life. It wasn't to be. *Former Taoiseach Bertie Ahern.*

Hearts and hours
We are at the end of a whole phase of capitalism, and now is the time for valuing things like time and love. *Journalist Veronica White.*

Braking the banks
These six institutions do not have any other friend in the EU or on the continent of Europe. *Minister for Finance Brian Lenihan as the Government covers the deposits and debts of six Irish financial institutions.*

This is the wrong solution to the wrong problem. It has put the Irish taxpayer at risk of considerable losses, and does nothing to solve the real problem of Irish banks, which is a shortage of capital. *Morgan Kelly, UCD professor of economics.*

When the Brits are whingeing we must be doing something right. *Property developer Noel Smyth.*

Les Irlandais éteignent l'incendie chez eux en se branchant sur la pompe à eau des voisins. [The Irish are putting out their fire by connecting up to their neighbours' pump.] *French MEP Alain Lamassoure.*

The cause of our problem was global so I can't say sorry with any type of confidence, sincerity and decency. But I do say a very genuine 'thank you' because that is right. *Seán Fitzpatrick, chairman, Anglo Irish Bank.*

In a wartime situation, we fight to defend ordinary people and this legislation is about defending ordinary business people, PAYE workers and people on social welfare. Unfortunately, I must support it with gritted teeth because there are a lot of scum, and I state this deferentially in one sense, who do not deserve to be bailed out in this way. *Green Party TD Paul Gogarty berates the bankers.*

Final solution
When the country's rich, what do people do? They go out and drink. When the country's poor, what do people do? They go out and drink. So one way or another, hopefully we'll come out okay. *John Mahon, promoter and publican.*

HERE & THERE
I clearly remember my mam saying to me and my two brothers when we were growing up: 'You're only English because you were born here.' And with a mother from Mayo and a father from Co. Meath, there's not a drop of English blood in me. *Oasis guitarist Noel Gallagher.*

Tongue-tied
We get people from everywhere here. We try to learn the basics in as many languages as we can to greet them. One guy here has phrases in about 15 languages. He puts the rest of us to shame. I only know a couple. *Dublinia tour guide Richie Murphy.*

Cut above . . .
The College of Surgeons is the first thing that Malaysians say when you mention you are from Ireland. It's the country's best brand here. *Brendan Lyons, president, Penang Medical College.*

Squiggle room
I'd encourage all those who have had negative experiences with B&Bs in the past, with squiggly carpets and nylon sheets, to try them out again. *Kate Burns, chairwoman, Town & Country Homes Association.*

Unidentified Fecking Object
What we have here is the best film of a UFO ever filmed in Ireland and perhaps some of the best footage ever captured worldwide. *Carl Nally, co-founder of UFO and Paranormal Research Ireland, on the achievement of a Co. Meath senior garda beyond the call of duty.*

Thar lear
The Irish immigrant centres all over the US are reporting a significant surge . . . and the anecdotal evidence in Irish neighbourhoods is

backing that up. We are particularly seeing the traditional type of Irish emigrant—construction workers, waitresses ... *Niall O'Dowd, founder member of the Irish Lobby for Immigration Reform.*

We were amazed at the sheer numbers of Irish-Americans who attended. It was a touching, moving, magnificent ceremony, and for the family, and all our supporters, it is just so great to finally have closure. *Julia Schayer, daughter of Annie Moore from Cork, first emigrant through Ellis Island, at the unveiling of a headstone over her hitherto unmarked New York grave.*

It's incredible that you can travel 4,000 miles from the White House and find such a fitting tribute to a man whose contribution to the early growth of the American capital was so immense. *White House curator Bill Allman at the opening of the James Hoban Memorial Arbour at Cuffesgrange, Co. Kilkenny.*

We'll see how I like America and how America likes me. *Charlie Bird on his appointment as RTÉ Washington correspondent.*

One that got away
This American came stamping down the stairs demanding, 'What's that goddamn fish doing up on that goddamn tower anyway?' I told him a very involved story about the salmon always swimming one foot under the water's surface, and the total height of Shandon being one foot less than the depth of the water at the time of the flood when Noah's Ark sailed around here. He was quite happy with that. *Declan Kelly, curator, St Anne's, Shandon, Cork City.*

The crane has flown
This crane was part of the history of the docks and was an important symbol of our industrial past. We need to ask the Docklands Authority and Dublin Port who removed it, and we can put in a freedom of information request if needs be ... *Labour councillor Kevin Humphries on the trail of a nineteenth-century artefact 'missing' from Dublin's dockland.*

Dragging their feet
We are slow now to fully pedestrianise streets because anti-social behaviour can occur. If people know that a car could come around the

next corner, that behaviour is less likely to occur, so we don't see letting cars through streets as completely detrimental. *Eoghan Madden, senior traffic engineer, Dublin City Council.*

Thought for food
The haunting memory of the Great Famine of the mid-nineteenth century still shapes Ireland's commitment to defeating global hunger and has made it a leader in the global fight against hunger. *Former UN secretary-general Kofi Annan.*

Vintage port
The visit of the QE2 here has been hugely nostalgic for Cobh. Cunard has links here going back to the 1890s and all the company's great ships would have come here at some stage or other over the years—it really does recall the glory days of transatlantic liners. *Captain Michael McCarthy, Port of Cork commercial manager, on the vessel's farewell visit.*

Puff
The north-west rail lobby is now gathering a head of steam and with this issue now firmly on the political agenda, lobbying on the issue will be intensified in the time ahead. *Pat Doherty MP on moves to extend the Belfast-Derry line into Donegal.*

CRIME & PUNISHMENT
As far as the accused people are concerned, they walk from this court today innocent of the charges laid against them. However, I hope they understand that, in life, people may be bullies in their own society, but they'll discover very quickly that there are bigger bullies around and I really hope the people of Waterford don't get up in a few weeks' or a few months' time to find one of you has been found in the back of a ditch with your hands tied behind your back with Sellotape and a bullet in your head. That's where you're headed, gentlemen. *Judge Rory McCabe warns two brothers acquitted of serious assault.*

I watched him and the other witnesses decline to give evidence in the trial, having initially given very damning statements to gardaí. These young people all gave the same message with fear written all over their face and embedded in their composure. I have no doubt as to the source of that fear. *Judge Frank O'Donnell, imposing a ten-year sentence for serious harm.*

Flaming disgrace

This is a despicable and outrageous act. To think that while firemen are out risking their lives on behalf of their community you have scumbags breaking into the fire station and stealing their belongings is beyond belief or comprehension. *Co. Wicklow Councillor John Brady.*

GAME ON

If that was Steve Staunton or Brian Kerr or Mick McCarthy, he'd be getting plenty of welly. And he'd deserve plenty of welly. He's way out of order. *Journalist Eamon Dunphy disapproves of Giovanni Trapattoni's team selection.*

I like messing with the press. When I use a sentence I use a lot of metaphors and they don't understand. In Germany I used to say, it's just 90 minutes of football, it is not a war! *Giovanni Trapattoni.*

Kangarules

Whenever this game is played right, whenever we play it right, it's probably as close to Gaelic football as we can make it. *Seán Kavanagh, Ireland's International Rules captain.*

That's not an international outlet for Gaelic games, and someone needs to stand up and say that. We should be promoting Gaelic games on a world stage, and if that has to start at club level, so be it. *Tyrone manager Mickey Harte.*

We believe the relationship between the two nations and the two different codes needs to be fostered and encouraged and we believe in making individuals accountable for their actions and they will be . . . if you are a competitor within and you love testing yourself there is no better concept. *Nathan Buckley, assistant coach and former Australian captain.*

Inner circle

You can't think how to hula-hoop. You've just got to feel it. *Mardyke del Castillo, circus skills tutor at Belfast's Crescent Arts Centre.*

Pit stop

It's been a hell of an experience. It was like driving a Formula One car at 160 miles an hour, stopping it dead and climbing out of it. You're standing back, still looking at the track, but there's nothing happening. *Former Ireland rugby manager Eddie O'Sullivan contemplates his retirement.*

Hitting the fan

The public are quite fickle at the moment. Angry fans are allowed forums by newspapers and internet sites where they hide behind pseudonyms and slate managers and players. It's unfair and in that regard the media have to show more responsibility and control. *Tyrone football manager Mickey Harte.*

Law of the jungle

You've got to understand that there's a huge difference between me winning a major and Tiger winning a major. From his earliest days it's what he was destined to do . . . *Champion golfer Pádraig Harrington.*

Losing the run

I'm retired today. It's my last run. I've arthritis in both feet and I'm sick of it. It's time to go playing football with the young lad, I think, and drink a few pints. *Michael O'Connor (35), first Irishman home in the Dublin Marathon, embraces the future.*

DE MORTUIS

Very good. Feel these people got what they deserved. They weren't saints. *DUP councillor Ian Stevenson visits Kilmainham Jail.*

Fond farewells

Irish people have a strong love for remembering their dead as seen by attendance at wakes, putting memorials into newspapers and sending out memorial cards. They now have the opportunity to tell the life story of their loved ones in a very visual and interactive way, and record it for future generations to appreciate. *Mr McGuiggan, co-director of the Derry-based Library Service Executive, inaugurates Ireland's first online memorial site.*

Funerals last about three days, arguments last about three years, which leads to more funerals. Travellers do funerals the old-fashioned traditional way. Travellers have great respect for the dead and so little for the living that they put all their energy into them. They make a huge effort with weddings too, but that's a form of getting rid of someone! *Traveller comedian Martin 'Beanz' Ward.*

Pull the other one
Previous attendees have felt the presence of a small boy and girl who like to play pranks on the visitors by pulling at their coats and/or hair. *Warren Coates of the Northern Ireland Paranormal Research Association on the supernatural attractions of Richhill Castle, Co. Armagh.*

Happy medium
When I walked in the door I went very cold and saw a little man with no hair who greeted us. I don't know what the history is here, or if he walks the grounds. I get the feeling, though, he was a good man, maybe a priest or a doctor, here to help sick people. There's so much activity here it's amazing. *Cork City Gaol rewards British spirit-seeker Tom Flynn.*

Unhappy returns
One theory of 'guising' and dressing as ghosts may be in the notion that the dead are returning on this night [Hallowe'en] and the change of appearance may protect the human from being recognised by the returning spirits of the dead. *Ms Butler, Department of Folklore and Ethnology, UCC.*

ARTS AND PARTS
Everyone with an accordion and a drum became a showband in 1969. *Singer and showband pioneer Brendan Bowyer.*

Mute inglorious Miltons
If poets went on strike, nobody would notice for 300 years, and then there would be a big black hole at the heart of our culture. *Paula Meehan at the Poetry Ireland 30th birthday celebrations.*

Blame not the Bard
It is not meant to be very funny. It's a tragedy. But we work with the concept of putting it in a setting that allows the humour to come out.

The Wild West has so many stereotypes that people recognise, such as the shoot-out, the Indians, and the bar brawls. They all have a place in the play. We were able to turn the duels in *Romeo and Juliet* into shoot-outs and brawls. *Marcus Bale, co-adapter of a Cork production aimed at teenagers.*

Even though Shakespeare and U2 are nearly 400 years apart, there's such a similarity in the language they use. They share common themes too, which include love and loss, heartbreak and politics. *Matt Walker, creator of us musical* As U2 Like It.

Pas de danse
I thought it would be easy to establish a ballet company, that people would jump in because they'd see that that was what was missing from their culture. That was my mistake. *Günther Falusy, co-founder of Ballet Ireland.*

Stamp of approval
Stamp-collecting was my childhood hobby. Little did I think that, one day, I might become a collectible myself. *Planxty's Andy Irvine, featured on an An Post series celebrating traditional music.*

Hanging judgment
People shouldn't forget that 50 people died over the period of the hunger strikes, 35 of them murdered by Republicans and 32 of those murdered by the IRA. I hope this isn't Republican propaganda; I hope this is properly contextualised. *Former Presbyterian moderator Rev. John Dunlop attends the Belfast premiere of* Hunger, *based on the last six weeks in the life of Bobby Sands.*

I'm dying to see what Cork audiences think of *Hunger*. I love going back to Cork, to hearing them say, 'I don't know what all the fuss is about.' You're always sure of that response in Cork. *Enda Walsh, who scripted the film.*

Undead
Horror is one of the most successful genres in cinema, and its appeal has lasted right up to the present day, but we're trying to recreate the genre on stage and the really exhilarating thing is that the illusion is

live—live and dangerous, happening in front of you—and that makes it more scary. *Riverdance producer John McColgan on his new theatrical venture.*

'This ad, you see. Keyes, you see.'

It's surprising how many writers have spent some part of their early lives in advertising. Mr Leopold Bloom sells advertising, doesn't he? That's what he's doing on Bloomsday. *Salman Rushdie, former copywriter.*

Switched on

I use pen and paper because I love the physical act of writing—and that you can sit down anywhere and do it longhand without worrying about low batteries or internet connections. I can write pretty much anywhere. *Novelist Cecelia Ahern.*

Gospel sleuth

It started out as a book for children, and developed from there. Simms asked us to write down every question we had about the book. How did they make the inks, which came from thousands of miles away? How did they produce the calf's vellum? What was the lifestyle of the monks? He arrived with the whole thing hand-written in green ink and read it aloud to us. *Publisher Michael O'Brien launching a Japanese translation of Archbishop George Simms' guide to the Book of Kells, which has sold 200,000 copies.*

Honour without profit

If you think about it, as somebody said to me recently, Daniel [Day-Lewis] and I winning the Oscars and coming to Ireland restarted the film industry in Ireland. We were personally responsible for getting it going again. You'd think they would be aware of this at least and try to include you in it. But it's the opposite. They just cut you dead. It's very odd and hurtful. *Actress Brenda Fricker.*

FAITH & MORALS

A number of years ago, I asked a father what he wanted for his son. He said he wanted him to have a sense of self-confidence without a sense of superiority. This is something very different to many other schools. *Fr Martin Daly, principal, Catholic University School, Dublin.*

Dermotology

Ted is an everyman. He has the twin obsessions that many of us have—money and fame—and he's a great man for justifying something dodgy such as fixing the raffle for the car or ripping off a song for the Eurovision. But there is a lot of loyalty there for his little 'family' on Craggy Island and we see that when he decides not to leave them for America. *Rev. Darren McCallig, Church of Ireland chaplain, Trinity College Dublin, on his sermon on 'The Gospel according to Fr Ted'.*

Rí-raw

We seem to be living through the death throes of raw capitalism (please God) with its appalling greed, recklessness, lack of accountability and complete disregard for any ethical behaviour and the consequences of that for ordinary hardworking people's lives, especially the poor. *Fr Godfrey O'Donnell, head of the Romanian Orthodox church in Ireland.*

PARTY LINES

An agreed agenda means you have an agenda agreed, which means you have agreed papers between the First and Deputy First Minister. *Gerry Kelly, NI Junior Minister, Sinn Féin.*

Never the twain

Northern Ireland needs action from Government now to help people through this very difficult time. However, the Executive won't even meet. This is an insult to local people and is a real snub in their time of need. *Alliance Party leader David Ford.*

Gerry Adams' comments are to be treated more in pity than in scorn. They betray a fundamentally sectarian mindset. Not only does he fail to comprehend that unionism is not a religion but that it is also possible to be a Roman Catholic and a unionist at the same time. *First Minister Peter Robinson responds to accusations of DUP anti-Catholic bigotry.*

Then there was none

When my end came it was almost like a release. The whole leadership change-over and the election had been very stressful. I just thought maybe it would be better if we all go out together. There was that feeling, 'We have gone down to two. This is not sustainable.' *Former Progressive Democrat minister Liz O'Donnell on her election defeat.*

Orange glow

We in government recognise the important cultural significance of bonfires within various community celebrations throughout Northern Ireland. We do not want to undermine tradition. However, we cannot overlook the fact that they have increasingly become environmental liabilities, stacked with heavily polluting tyres and wooden pallets. *Environment minister Sammy Wilson promoting bea-cons as an alternative to the customary conflagrations.*

SOCIAL & PERSONAL

As a small child it was like a fairytale growing up in this building but there were times in my life when it was very uncomfortable. For someone who was born in Dublin and brought up in Slane, Co. Meath, to be accused by some of being a 'west Brit' was pretty goddamn offensive and at a period even threatening. *Lord Henry Mountcharles of Slane Castle.*

Tie break

We don't normally sit on Friday. I always dress down on a Friday and will continue to do so. As for having to wear a tie, I think that should be up to the individual. *Labour Senator Dominic Hannigan, admonished by the Captain of the Guard on the matter of sartorial rectitude.*

Time, gentlemen

People have 12-hour days, taking trains to Dublin and not getting back till 7 p.m. or 8 p.m. By the time they have something to eat and see the family, the idea of a bit of a spin to the pub is not something most people are going to do. *PJ Kavanagh, Kavanagh's pub, Portlaoise, Co. Laois.*

Rubber stamp

That's a huge problem. It's probably going back to gender norms, and how women are supposed to behave. If I am seen to be ready for sex in this way, does it have an impact on my reputation? *Caroline*

Spillane, director, Crisis Pregnancy Agency, on the reluctance of young women to carry condoms.

Life of spice
I'm very conscious that I don't want to become someone like David Beckham and Posh Spice and the people that seek that kind of life-style. My whole belief system would be completely contrary to that. *Munster and Ireland rugby star Ronan O'Gara.*

Stickin' out
There's no denying we are a dour people. We don't attract sympathy. We're stubborn, pigheaded, and compromise does not come easy to us. *Former Ulster Democratic Unionist Party member David Adams characterises his fellow Northern Protestants.*

All fired up
Robert and I went to the debs in a fire engine, along with three other couples, which was great as we were able to stand up and dance in it on the way to the debs. *Dublin student Nicola Donnan.*

Last laugh
Sudden death during laughing just does not happen. There are very few people who die laughing. There is some unknown element there. *Psychiatrist Dr Bill Fry reassures UCC students.*

LISBONIANA
There might be those who will want to go ahead on their own, but I think it is totally unrealistic. Nobody wants to see Ireland out of the EU and this is certainly not the wish of the Irish people. *EU commissioner Margot Wallström.*

The ins and outs
To me it is shocking that a government that held a referendum and failed is still in office. A government that puts a question to a referendum and loses has to resign: that's democracy. *Spanish MEP Íñigo Méndez de Vigo.*

Brussels clouts

It manifested itself in almost physical ways. It may be the perception of these things, but they looked shrunken. They looked like beaten people. *RTÉ's Europe editor, Seán Whelan, on the impact of the No vote on Irish civil servants working in Brussels.*

Play it again, Sam

We cannot wait for Godot because Godot never comes. *Romanian MEP Adrian Severin loses patience with Ireland's indecision.*

HE STEPPED IN AND HE STEPPED OUT AGAIN

This budget serves no vested interest. Rather, it provides an opportunity for us all to pull together and play our part according to our means so that we can secure the gains which have been the achievement of the men and women of this country. It is, a Cheann Comhairle, no less than a call to patriotic action. *Brian Lenihan, Minister for Finance.*

My patriotism does not include hammering the elderly, the sick, the disabled, and young children in large classes. *Finian McGrath TD.*

Class extinction

In situations such as this, the inevitable results are the narrowing of the curriculum, the amalgamation of classes, and even the dropping of subjects in an education system where we are already concerned at the low numbers of graduates in science and mathematics. This will be the death knell on our inspirations of becoming a knowledge society. *Peter McMenamin, General Secretary, Teachers' Union of Ireland.*

Much drama and, quite frankly, hysteria, has been whipped up about protecting our children's future and the impact, in particular, of increases in class size. I'm from Cork, a county that knows a thing or two about hurling . . . But Ruairi Quinn, who this morning refused to say where he'd make the savings, is the most skilful hurler on the ditch I've ever encountered. *Minister for Education Batt O'Keeffe.*

Labour's love lost

Ministers will congratulate themselves on their 'tough love approach' but will Brian Cowen be able to look in the eye of a family whose livelihood has been destroyed by his economic mismanagement and say to them, 'I feel your pain'? Like hell you will. *Labour spokeswoman on finance Joan Burton.*

Air waived
There were only two paragraphs talking about the removal of medical cards from the over-70s. We had no other information. We only discovered about it at four o'clock the following afternoon. It left us in a vacuum. *Fianna Fáil TD Noel O'Flynn.*

Blythe spirit
This act will be remembered, and not just for this generation. Brian Lenihan will go down as the man who took medical care from the old, sick and vulnerable of this country. *Dr James Reilly, Fine Gael health spokesman.*

Sticking point
It's a pure disaster in the world. I could not go to a funeral and go out the door but people were sticking into me. The one thing they do not want to hear the word of is 'means test'. A lot of them feel if there's a means test then their pensions will be taken away. I cannot vote against the old people. *Independent TD Jackie Healy-Rae.*

If he had come on and said: 'Look, I have made a terrible mistake. I'm really sorry. There is a problem and we are going to do everything we can to sort it out. We are rethinking it. We are going to rectify it.' But no. Waffling. I know bugger-all about Irish politics but on the basic principle of how you look after the old, it is the same wherever you go surely. *British broadcaster Michael Parkinson.*

When you are old and grey ...
My take on it is that the Celtic Tiger was jumping around out there the last few years, and all the grey panthers were hidden out there afraid of the tiger. With the tiger gone, they are no longer afraid to come out and out they came with their sticks, on their frames and in wheelchairs. Looking at the crowds on the street this week made me feel proud to be old. *Kevin Molloy, head of Active Retirement Ireland, on the over-70s' protest against the planned withdrawal of the Medical Card.*

I think a lot of people are frightened. We are being penalised for having paid our taxes and our insurance all our lives. I don't think it's fair. I don't think it's right. *Tony Goodwin (75), Glenaulin Nursing Home, Dublin.*

I don't want a medical card. What would I want with one of them? I don't want children's allowance either but I still get it. That's what's all wrong with this country. *Ryanair chief executive Michael O'Leary.*

I have only one word for taking away our cards and that is euthanasia. I am so mad. *Marjorie Parker (72) at the protest meeting in St Andrew's church, Dublin.*

If it was a younger age-group the whole country would be up in arms, if that amount of people were allowed into a Catholic church to behave in such a manner. *Senator Geraldine Feeney.*

I have no problem apologising for the behaviour in the church. It was just the anger that was voiced and probably some of the people weren't listened to, but I suppose you have to understand the great anger that people were experiencing. *Fr John Gilligan, administrator, St Andrew's.*

BIN THERE . . .
It was very weird as every wheelie bin in the town was from my home town. *Dubliner Aidan Pedreschi, on a round-the-world charity cycle, discovers Fingal County Council bins in residence in Lovrin, Romania.*

November 2008

I could see this thing coming

says RTÉ's economic editor George Lee: 'Anybody who didn't have their heads stuck in the sand could see it coming. So why do we say now that we are suddenly hit by something which we never saw coming and we're in it together?' The obsession with the recession gathers force and the fallout from the budget débâcle doesn't go away. Nail bars and hair salons feature in the falling from grace of state agency Fás. The Progressive Democrats finally bow to the inevitable while the National Socialist Party makes an unscheduled Dáil appearance. Cliché of the Month: 'credit crunch'.

HEIL LEO! *Conor Lenihan, Minister for Integration, salutes Fine Gael's Leo Varadkar.*

I did not call anyone a fascist. I said his policies were associated with the British fascist party. *Conor Lenihan.*

There was a Nazi salute too. Deputies cannot make Nazi salutes in this chamber. *Fergus O'Dowd TD.*

The man's an idiot. That's all that can be said about it. *Malcolm Lewis, president, the Dublin Jewish Progressive Congregation.*

O'BAMA
We're hopeful that, come Wednesday morning, Brian Cowen will be congratulating US president-elect Barack Obama and inviting him to the town of his ancestors. *Canon Stephen Neill, Moneygall, Co. Offaly.*

The only thing that seems to happen around here is car crashes, but this will change things. We're absolutely delighted. *Moneygall resident Moira Sheppard.*

The last time I saw this excitement was when we won the senior county hurling in 1975. We're only a small little parish and how proud we are. *Moneygall resident Ollie Larkin.*

I have no doubt he'll go to Ireland during the course of his presidency. I know he's aware of his own Irish heritage and he has a deep affection for the Irish. *Massachusetts congressman William Delahunt.*

I'll go out and brief Obama, fly back with him and introduce him to all the local characters. My contacts in the White House tell me that, subject to FBI clearance, Brian Cowen will be allowed to cross the border into North Tipp on the big day. *Michael Lowry TD.*

PARTY LINES
It is clear that Mary Hanafin and her cabinet colleagues have no idea what they are doing and, at this stage, Fianna Fáil stands for 'flip-flop'. *Fine Gael TD Olwyn Enright perceives another Budget U-turn.*

Following the recent Budget, RTÉ had all left-wing commentators on programmes without balance. Audiences were loaded against Government representatives. *Fianna Fáil TD Noel Treacy.*

Never have so few people annoyed so many for so few results. *Former Fine Gael leader Alan Dukes sums up the Budget.*

Brian Lenihan is a barrister. Maybe if he'd spent more time in the King's Inns reading Cicero he could have avoided his run-in with the elderly in the Budget. *Professor Colm Kenny discovers a hitherto unknown copy of* De Senectute *in the Law Library.*

Some achieve greatness . . .
The role of political leadership in Northern Ireland was not a role that we were gifted. It is one that we earned. We earned it by winning the trust of the unionist electorate. *NI First Minister Peter Robinson.*

Look at the pitiful sight of Peter Robinson over recent weeks. The Provos bring the same blackmail and bully-boy tactics to government as they used for decades on the streets through bombing and murder, and all the 'joint First Minister' can do is wag his 'bad dog' finger and threaten 'serious consequences', and the dog responds by barking in his face and eyeing him up as a suitable lamppost. *Traditional Unionist Voice leader Jim Allister.*

PeeDeeatrics

When we were formed, Des O'Malley was a year younger than Obama is today. Bobby Molloy had six successive elections behind him. Pearse Wyse had five and I had three. In order for the party to continue, you need people of that calibre that have a political track record. I don't see that in the party today. *Former Progressive Democrat leader Mary Harney.*

I want to stay on. I'm not just somebody that gives up lightly. I enjoy the job. I want to do the job for as long as I have the energy to do it and clearly the support of the Taoiseach in doing it. *Mary Harney faces the future.*

She has no mandate, no party and no accountability. Her position has long been untenable. Now, however, she is in a dangerous position. She has no mandate; she is not facing the electorate again—so she can do what she wants. *Cancer specialist Professor John Crown.*

Out, out, out

Gerry Adams is yesterday's man—out of step, out of tune, out of touch, out of excuses. But he hasn't gone away you know, and now he's doing what he does best—threatening and bullying anyone who gets in his way. *NI Minister of Finance Nigel Dodds.*

Few human beings of my acquaintance are as petty and mean-spirited and negative as those in the Afrikaaner wing of unionism. *Gerry Adams at a fund-raising dinner in New York.*

AN t-AOS ÓG

There was a great saying, 'I'll go anywhere within reason, but I won't go home.' There was a bit of that when I was younger. Young people should be able to go out and enjoy themselves. My only advice would be just to keep the head basically. *An Taoiseach Brian Cowen.*

Thought for food

The foreign lads, that's the way they've been brought up. The English lads are not too bad. The biggest problems are the Irish and Scottish players. That's because of how they're brought up. That's how I was, eating rubbish, drinking rubbish. It's trying to change that mentality. *Soccer manager and former player Roy Keane.*

Upper crust

We were brought up by nannies and nursery maids, and lived on the top floor, which wasn't finished—money ran out in the late 18th century and some of the rooms weren't plastered and had no ceilings. We didn't see our parents much. *The Knight of Glin's childhood in Glin Castle, Co. Limerick.*

Reality check

Towards the end of my duty it started to rain heavily and then I went into the bunker to try and get some sleep. It was very smoky and, after 10 p.m., the only lights were the fires outside. It was very realistic. You don't really understand what it was like until you do something like this. And we were doing it just one night. Can you imagine doing it day after day for years? *Cian O'Connell (16) endures a re-enactment of 1914-18 trench warfare.*

Inhuman rites

To send these two young girls back to an environment where they may be threatened with female genital mutilation, which has already claimed the life of an older sister, raises serious concerns about the Government's commitment to children. *Jillian van Turnhout, chief executive, Children's Rights Alliance.*

The barbaric idea that two young girls could be subjected to this awful practice and that Ireland does not intervene, I believe, it's not reflecting the will of the vast majority of people in this country who want to see Pamela Izevbekhai being allowed to stay in this country with her two children. *Fine Gael Senator Frances Fitzgerald.*

I will do whatever I have to, to protect my girls. I can't blame those who don't understand my situation or don't know about the reality of life for women like me. *Nigerian mother Pamela Izevbekhai.*

STUPID ECONOMY

I know we all want a head on the plate or blood on the table but that's not always the appropriate solution either. Everything is perfect in hindsight. This recession will remain longer if everybody keeps concentrating on trying to make scapegoats for what happened in the past. EU *commissioner Charlie McCreevy.*

It's like the Irish are experiencing a tsunami. We have gone through the first waves of this crisis, but we still do not know how bad it is going to be or when it will come to an end. People are feeling vulnerable and powerless. How well each individual weathers this storm will vary considerably. *Psychotherapist Brighid Daly Connolly.*

No. Absolutely not. Nobody has spoken to me about taking a cut in salary. I know the argument is, you're meant to be showing leadership, but that's not the solution. *Broadcaster Gerry Ryan demurs.*

Cause and effect

My Irish colleague Brian Crowley has said here today that it's the banks' fault that we are in the mess we are in. He blames bankers for acting like bankers and seeking to maximise short-term profit to the limits of the law. MEP *Proinsias de Rossa addresses the European Parliament in Strasbourg.*

The midweek drinking has dried up, people are getting more focused. There's a terror of failing or dropping out. I've stopped driving to college because I can't afford the petrol. It costs me nearly €30 to get home in a taxi at night—I could fly to London for less. *Georgie Gavin, student, Dublin Business School.*

Break for the Border

I love shopping and I have enjoyed my trans-Atlantic trip to shop in New York as much as the next woman. But these are critical times. People need to be aware that when they make the decision to go North they are taking their spending out of the city and there will be repercussions. *Dublin Lord Mayor Eibhlin Byrne.*

To be honest, I'll be shopping wherever I can get the best value for money and I'll continue to do so as long as Irish consumers continue to be ripped off. *Radio presenter Claire Byrne.*

There is one commodity where the differentials are unforgivably high and that is basic foods and that is why most people are going to Newry. Mary Coughlan needs to get her arse around a proper review of the supply chain which brings things into Ireland. *Bill Tosh, Dundalk Chamber of Commerce.*

Lowering the boom
Those who questioned the boom—its foundations, its longevity, the uses to which it was being put—were decried as everything from anti-national to puritanical. And now that it's gone, perhaps it's time that the voices of those who were silenced through embarrassment, inadequacy or bullying during the boom may now be heard. *Ombudsman Emily O'Reilly.*

In your fancy take flight
I've no interest in aviation. To me, an airplane is a bus with wings on it. It's just a business. I was hopeful I could make money at it and at the same time provide services to the regions of Ireland that are entitled to those services. I've made some money. *Pádraig Ó Céidigh, owner, Aer Arann.*

Post script
I looked at her with my mouth open. '£21. It is a birthday card I am sending to Navan, Ireland, not the USA,' I said. She said there was nothing she could do but that was the price. *Newry man Tony Carroll learns of the Royal Mail charge for next-day delivery.*

LISBONIANA
Corrective measures are always possible—we have to be just patient and just ask this question once more when you are ready. *Latvian president Valdis Zatlers in Limerick.*

Sweet clarity
It is as clear as a pikestaff that at the end of the day Ireland will be left with a stark choice: either ratify the treaty or join the slow-speed Europe. *Michael Mulcahy TD.*

On-hands approach
Sinn Féin has offered to work with the Taoiseach to address the many key issues of concern to the electorate, particularly in the areas of

workers' rights, public services, tax sovereignty and democracy. But Brian Cowen seems intent instead to sit on his hands waiting for a solution to drop out of the sky, or, as it now seems, until President Sarkozy tells him what to do. *MEP Mary Lou McDonald.*

The eyes have it
The Irish people have eyes and ears. They can clearly see the truth of Ireland's position in Europe, and they can also see that the people they have elected would rather that they did not have all of the facts. *Libertas spokeswoman Caroline Simons.*

Take me to your leader
I'm at the disposal of Declan Ganley to enable this large pan-European movement to be present in France, and if he chooses me as one of his representatives I would be very glad to accept. *Philippe de Villiers, Mouvement pour la France.*

This man hasn't a whiff of anything off him that I can see and I can see a CIA man at 50 yards. *Eamon Dunphy finds no fault with the Libertas leader.*

As long as it takes
It certainly makes things a bit more difficult for Turkey, but Turkey doesn't look for membership next year or in two years' time, so we hope that five to ten years from now the Irish will have ample time to reconsider. *Turkish economist Professor Sevet Paniuk.*

PAYING ON THE NAILS
I'm entitled to travel first class. *Fás chief executive Rody Molloy, responding to criticism of his organisation's expenditure on travel and ancillary indulgences.*

I am not standing over any profligate or unauthorised spending. No one can stand over that. *Taoiseach Brian Cowen.*

What on earth were the top brass in Fás doing, over looking at the space centre in Florida? I mean, do we have apprentice astronauts or something, or were they in the nail bar trying to register apprentices for carpentry? *Labour leader Eamon Gilmore.*

It's unfortunate the small amount of money that was probably paid for a hair-do has been caught up in a bigger bill, and there are questions about that bigger bill and how it came about. *Minister Mary Hanafin.*

I have no intention of spending the Order of Business discussing hairdos, pedicures or manicures. *Ceann Comhairle John O'Donoghue.*

One is learning on a daily basis of an almost bacchanalian looseness regarding public expenditure in the higher echelons of a State agency. *Senator Dan Boyle.*

Fás management said we were wasting our time going to the LRC and the decision was final, but we are determined to save these jobs if we can and to highlight the double standards it reveals about how ordinary Fás employees are treated compared with senior management. *SIPTU branch organiser Brendan O'Brien.*

Our economy is now in a fight for survival. We must not allow uninformed, populist, hypocritical or politically-motivated Puritanism to discourage those who are fighting for us on the front lines of job creation from doing what is necessary to win opportunity for our country in a shrinking but ever more competitive world market. *Former civil servant and diplomat Michael Lillis.*

MARRIAGE À LA MODE
Those who are committed to the probity of the Constitution, to the moral integrity of the word of God and to the precious human value of marriage between a man and a woman as the foundation of society may have to pursue all avenues of legal and democratic challenge to the published legislation if this is the case. *Cardinal Brady reacts to planned legislation to recognise cohabiting and same-sex couples.*

To make a totem of marriage in the way that it is being done is nothing other than blasphemous. I refer to the Gospel of Jesus Christ. When he was reprimanded by the Pharisees for breaking the Sabbath, he made the point that this was an institution made for man; that man was not made for the institution. *Senator David Norris.*

The economy and its values dominate current affairs programmes. What is happening to family, community, relationships no longer occupies the same place in society that it used to. *Fr Harry Bohan, chairman, the Céifin Centre.*

We are poised between a traditional assumption that children are protected best by keeping them ignorant of their parents' circumstances, and a newer idea that children need to know about and participate in family affairs if they are to cope with change. *Family law expert Geoffrey Shannon.*

It's very odd and strange. At this point in time when a huge number of births are to unmarried couples, this situation is at variance with the social norms of the country. It is not right for a doctor to impose certain moralities on patients. *Dr James Reilly TD queries a Galway fertility clinic's refusal to treat unmarried couples.*

DE MORTUIS
Ronnie was one of those people who, the more you got from them, the more you wanted. One story was never enough, one song, one album, one laugh and one life wasn't enough for Ronnie. We wanted more. One consolation is that we still have his music. It's not enough but it helps. *Brendan Gleeson. Ronnie Drew died in August 2008.*

Ronnie was a romantic, but he was acerbic too. He was well able to give you a bollicking. Even when we were doing the album and I'd drive him to the studio, I'd take considerable criticism over my driving. You'd almost think I'd tried to kill him a few times. *Aengus Fanning, editor, Sunday Independent.*

A LITTLE LEARNING
When it comes to education matters, Caitríona Ruane is about as confused as Adam on Mother's Day and is about as much use as a trap door on a canoe. *Mervyn Storey, chairman of the Stormont education committee, is less than impressed by his minister.*

Painless injection
Without getting specific about it, I love programmes which are underpinned by intelligence but which wear it lightly. There's nothing

like learning something without feeling like you're being taught and to have that delivered with wit and attitude. *Ana Leddy, head of RTÉ Radio 1.*

Town and gown
There is a tension between the traditional expectation that universities will primarily teach students, and the more recent requirement for universities to underpin economic development and attract corporate research and development into Ireland, not to mention the role of universities as agencies of cultural regeneration and of tackling disadvantage and structural poverty. *Professor Ferdinand von Prondzynski, Dublin City University.*

All mod. cons.
If the Minister could point out a single school in a worse condition than this one I'll stop shouting. If there is another school where the walls are cracked, where there is mould and damp everywhere, windows held together with nails and wire, where neither the storage heater, the toilets or the taps work properly and there are mice and rats, the principal of that school should get in touch with me and I will offer him or her my sympathies. *Elizabeth Mulry, principal, Eglish National School, Ahascragh, Co. Galway.*

ARTS & PARTS
The perversity of this is that weak arguments gain traction with repetition, and charismatic leaders of doubtful reputation are fêted by the media. It is a cranks' charter. *Willie O'Reilly, chairman, Independent Broadcasters of Ireland, finds fault with the requirement for equal airtime in referendum debates.*

Poor reception
Funnily enough I've been around all day today and nobody's even mentioned the bloody thing to me. It's probably a huge turn-off. I don't know if anyone is watching it. *Former Taoiseach Bertie Ahern on the RTÉ series devoted to his life and times.*

Clerical errors
There was an interview with us in a reputable English newspaper and it had something in it which none of us ever said. You're told that that

sort of thing only happens in other papers, not in reputable ones. The local parishioners find it all very amusing. 'Fame at your time of life?' seems to be a common refrain. *Fr Eugene O'Hagan of The Priests singing group.*

Dry run
I have always been interested in the Irish treaty debates so I decided to write a play about them. I am trying to condense the most interesting nine days of debate into two-and-a-half hours. *British Labour MP Andrew MacKinlay.*

Every Lidl helps
It's like Tesco, but easier. And there's no money changing hands, unless there are fines. You just put the card in and press the buttons. *South Dublin county librarian Ian Stobbart on his new online book-renewal facility.*

Country of the blind
There is a massive lack of visual awareness in Ireland. If you travel to Paris, for example, you sense a real awareness of architecture, even among taxi drivers, an awareness of the architects who are working in the city and of their work. You don't get that in Ireland, where creativity is more literary and theatre-based. *Architect Dave Flannery of Scott Tallon Walker.*

Brat pack
Never again work with children or animals. The animals were okay because they were dead, but the kids were very much alive. That was a total nightmare. It wore out everyone on the film. We would be ready to shoot a scene and Shane would have gone off in a bad mood or Kelly would have climbed a tree. *Lance Daly, long-suffering director of* Kisses, *a chronicle of Dublin street life.*

ONLY A GAME
Like other players on the European tour I found myself thinking that if Pádraig could win a major, so could I. Yet I don't think there's anyone in Europe in the same league as him where the mental side of the game is concerned. *Fellow golfer Darren Clarke.*

Handover

We played against each other a long time ago. It was nice. He saw me, I saw him so we shook hands, chatted for half an hour or so. He has the same problem in getting the players to adapt to the way he wants to play. *Former Republic of Ireland manager Jack Charlton meets current manager Giovanni Trapattoni.*

Hurlers ditched

The fundamental issue here is whether players have a right to effectively appoint their own managers or veto the appointment of managers. I don't believe they should. It is undesirable, unworkable and untenable. *Cork hurling manager Gerald McCarthy.*

They want to get rid of a certain section of us. Every statement that the board has made, everything, and Gerald is unfortunately taking the heat for the board, has been directed towards pressurising the younger guys. *Donal Óg Cusack, Cork goalkeeper.*

Surely in a county the size of Cork there are other guys who were capable of doing as good a job as Gerald did in the last two years. If Gerald was the guy afterwards, grand. All the county board had to do was to interview every fella and probably just say, grand, we all think Gerald McCarthy is the best man for the job. But no, they jumped the gun; they seemed to be saying 'fuck ye' to the players. *Seán Óg Ó hAilpín.*

I accept that Seán Óg has a very busy life. His substantial commercial interests arising from his Cork hurling career, dealing with his agent, his membership of the GPA, his job with the Ulster Bank must make it difficult to find time to reflect. If he did find time, then perhaps he wouldn't be flip-flopping around the place and changing his mind about my abilities as a coach to suit the agenda of the day. *Gerald McCarthy.*

Hazards of Oz

After Vintage Crop we thought they were going to come over here every year and win it, and we felt that was wrong, as it is an Aussie race. But now we know how difficult it is to travel here so we are more relaxed. I don't mind admitting I've pinched a lot of ideas from Aidan [O'Brien]. *Leading trainer Lee Freedman keeps a grip on the Melbourne Cup.*

If you are going to penalise me or the lads that's a nonsense. We have come here in good faith. *Aidan O'Brien rejects the accusation that he made use of pacemakers.*

While an international cap is welcome and the bonds with Australia are important the Railway Cup is suffering. This year it has been very badly hit because players are gone abroad playing a game that isn't even Gaelic football. *Connacht bainisteoir John O'Mahony.*

End games
Sometimes I'm asked how I switched over from GAA to rugby. Well in 1970 I was captain of the UCC Gaelic football team and we played at one end of the Mardyke and the rugby team played at the other end of the Mardyke. So how did I manage it? All I did was walk from one end to the other. *Former rugby international Moss Keane.*

I hated keeping goals because as far as I was concerned everyone else was out there enjoying themselves and I was stuck in a cage. *Veteran Irish goalkeeper and Munich disaster hero Harry Gregg.*

'ATIN' & DRINKIN'
There's no yelling in my kitchen. No abuse. I won't tolerate that kind of thing. I look after my staff. They are the greatest resource. *Blacklion, Co. Cavan restaurateur Neven Maguire.*

Core principle
The official asked to talk to me privately because the matter might be embarrassing. When I heard that, I didn't know what was going on. I was subsequently told the health officer wanted to know if it was true I was distributing unpasteurised apple juice around Co. Kildare. I had to reassure them that I was not distributing apple juice on a grand scale. *Junior Minister for Food Trevor Sargent.*

Spoon-fed
People see something on TV that shocks them but they convince themselves that the government has sorted it all out. People no longer consider themselves responsible for what they eat. They consider the government responsible for what they eat. It's an interesting phenomenon. *Co. Antrim organic farmer Tom Gilbert.*

Fruitless endeavour
They ripened really well this year, but sadly there will be no wine—the birds ate all the grapes. *Co. Dublin* vigneron *David Llewellyn.*

CRIME & PUNISHMENT
We cannot understand how we were propelled from our normal daily lives into such a national drama and shudder at the realisation that, had the plan been effected, we could have been poisoned to death. *Robert and Niall Howard, sons of PJ Howard, give their victim impact statement ahead of the sentencing of Sharon Collins for conspiracy to murder both them and their father.*

Sharon is, in my opinion, one of the nicest people you could ever have been fortunate to know. *PJ Howard.*

See no evil
Most people will be surprised to learn that the Garda currently has no legal powers to undertake electronic surveillance of criminal suspects, although those powers form a central part of the crime armoury of most countries. *Labour justice spokesman Pat Rabbitte.*

Gang aft a-gley
We always knew what these people were capable of doing, but they generally went out and murdered one another. Now they are murdering people without even checking to see if they are murdering the right people. *Limerick Mayor John Gilligan on the murder of Shane Geoghegan.*

You can pick up a newspaper and read who was the intended victim of this killing. You can read the gang that carried it out and some of the names of the gang members and the whereabouts of some of them. *Labour leader Eamon Gilmore.*

People involved in criminal activity cannot seem to stop. They are just on a different level and I wish they would open their hearts and their minds and think seriously about this, and I wish they would just stop this horrific continuation of crime. *Fr Tom Mangan, administrator, St Joseph's parish, Limerick.*

We have to be careful as there is a danger of making things worse: we saw what happened in England during the 1970s when governments took shortcuts with the law. The Birmingham Six, the Guildford Four, the Maguires. It won't make anything better if we start locking up innocent people. *James Hamilton, DPP, on agitation to reform the criminal law in the wake of gang violence.*

Both your houses

If the morons who seem to have a resentment and bitterness in them against either Orange halls or GAA halls see that the consequence of their attacks means there will be bigger and better premises built instead, maybe that will have an impact. *NI Culture and Leisure Minister Gregory Campbell.*

Dunlop tires

We always knew this day was coming. We will not be contesting the charges. *Frank Dunlop following his arrest by members of the Criminal Assets Bureau.*

HERE & THERE

We've almost 600 people on the waiting list in Killarney and to house bats before humans beggars belief. *Kerry County Councillor Donal Grady on the proposal to renovate a cottage on the Ring of Kerry for a family of bats.*

The pits

There are more fellas in this town working down holes in the street than you'd get in Calcutta. *Wicklow resident Jem Byrne.*

Location, location . . .

A lot of people who come here really do not know which country they are in—they just know they are out of their own country and are looking for protection. *Robin Hanan, chief executive, Irish Refugee Council.*

I felt I had come home when I first came here 20 years ago. I know a lot of English and Europeans feel the same about Ireland, but not all of them last the course. Some find they can't take the weather or the lack of a real work ethic—people here work to live, not live to work—but I love it. *Actor Jeremy Irons.*

Far green fields

It's a great networking and bonding structure. At the same time it provides lots of fun and fitness and opens up the Irish community to you. I know more Irish people as a result of the GAA after six years in China than I did after 25 years in London. *Angela Keane, Fás representative in China, on the GAA in Beijing.*

It was a real pleasure being with the Irish military in this fantastic camp. *French foreign minister Bernard Kouchner visits the UN force in Chad.*

It is foolish for Irish people to join foreign armies at a time when they are doing their fighting in places like Afghanistan. *Retired Army commandant and peace activist Edward Horgan.*

Nothing like a Dane

All the time, because we are a band of marauding Vikings, our aim is to sneak up on unsuspecting Celts and scare them. We look out for people who haven't seen us because they're talking on their mobile phones or busy reading maps. When we spot one we give them the Viking roar. It can scare the bejaysus out of them. *Rory O'Neill, amphibious driver and commentator, Dublin Viking Splash Tours.*

SOCIAL & PERSONAL

They are earthy, fiery, wild and sensual, and above all they have that glint in their eye. You can't find it anywhere else. *Former Miss Ireland Jakki Moore's verdict on the Irish male.*

But I was ridiculed by the ordinary people in my hometown when photos of me in a bikini first appeared. I met the parish priest soon after and he sneered: 'Oh, so this is the infamous Nuala Holloway.' It was so unfair and small-minded. And you know, it was tame compared to what you see now. *Another former Miss Ireland.*

Hooked shot

If Eamon ever went to school without boots, it's probably because he was too big for them. *George 1 Eamon 0.*

Arresting embrace

Iris Robinson is a regular customer and has frequently sat beside the kissing policemen. *Sam Spain, owner of Belfast's Gourmet Burger restaurant, defending his controversial wall hanging.*

Bono publico

He gives everyone the time of day. He finds it hard to say 'no' if anyone comes up to talk or ask him for a picture. There are plenty of photos out there with his arms around big fat men too—it's just that none of these make the paper. *Artist Guggi on his friend Bono being photographed with two bikini-clad ladies.*

Hippocratic vote

Fifty years from now, it will not be important what my bank account was. It will not be important what kind of car I drove, nor will it be important what size of house I lived in. But it does matter to me that during my stay in this House, I may have been, just may have been, important in the life of a child. *Dr Jim McDaid TD refusing to support a government withdrawal of a proposed cervical cancer vaccine distribution scheme.*

LOST WORD

Economic Teutonic plates have just shifted comprehensively. *Gerry Howlin, former adviser to former Taoiseach Bertie Ahern.*

Will there be money to feed the pigs for Christmas?

asks Mitchelstown pig farmer Rory O'Brien: 'There is the possibility of the biggest meltdown of intensive Irish agriculture in years. This is about survival for pig farmers.' Meltdown is averted, as is the dioxin threat, but not before something like panic sets in among Full Irish Breakfast fanciers. Financial meltdown remains, however, a real prospect, with Lisbon the resident pachyderm in the apartment. Cliché of the Month: 'road map' (esp. Dublin–Lisbon; also useful for 'going forward', 'out there').

If you take a capsule of cyanide, you'll drop down dead. If you did the same with a sausage, you're not going to. But if you're eating sausages every day of your life with these levels of dioxins, you might end up in very poor health. *Alan Reilly, Food Safety Authority of Ireland.*

In sausages and pudding, so many pieces of so many pigs are commingled, there's no way of tracing that back. You could trace it back to the day of manufacture but you couldn't trace it back to the individual farmer. *Brendan Lynch, head of pig services, Teagasc.*

When we had the Mad Cow it soon got sorted out, so there's no point in making a big deal. *Elizabeth Cox, Santry, Co. Dublin.*

The whole production cycle is very efficient. The pigs just have to move on—it's not like cattle where you can move them to another field for a few weeks and they'll be alright. They get too heavy and then they're not valuable any more. *Amii Cahill, Irish Farmers' Association.*

Pigs back?
It was a case of all hands on deck to get the product off the shop floor. I would hope they can flush this all through quite quickly and get safe

product back on sale. It's an awful time for this to happen when we're already struggling to keep sales up. *Pat Stapleton, Tesco store manager, Merrion Road, Dublin.*

Pork is bad for pains, though I'm not sure why. I always eat beef sausages. *Customer Norah McCullagh, Crowe's butchers, Belfast.*

CHURCH & STATE
In the early days it was the most difficult situation. You are in a place where people speak the same language as you but are in conflict with you. Contrast that to, say, the Falklands, where it was very different— you knew where the threat was coming from and you had a defined enemy. *Major General Chris Brown, relinquishing his posting as last general officer commanding the British army in Northern Ireland.*

Fallen idol
Of course there is an obsession with Haughey; he is dead for three years and he was last Taoiseach in 1992, which is 16 years ago, and the events that are being rehearsed now are more than a quarter of a century old. We should move on. *PJ Mara, his former adviser, on allegations that Haughey had spread rumours concerning President Hillery's private life.*

The name of CJ was magic. He was idolised and loved by the plain people of Ireland. *John O'Mahony, chairman of the National Museum of Ireland, accepting the gift to the State of Haughey's 4,000-volume library.*

Singular pluralism
Have we really forgotten what Christmas is all about? I sincerely hope there is room in legislation on broadcasting currently before the Oireachtas that will see an end to bizarre interpretation of rules around religious advertising. *Archbishop Diarmuid Martin on the banning of a TV commercial for Veritas, the church-owned religious goods outlet.*

It sounds a bit crazy. There's a little touch of anything to do with religion being no longer acceptable. This so-called pluralist Ireland might be pluralist for everybody except somebody who's speaking reason about Christmas. *Fr Enda McDonagh, former professor of moral theology, Maynooth.*

Religious intent
I went to a Redeemed Church convention out in Ratoath in July and it was the largest group of Christians I've ever been a part of. In one sitting there were about 10,000 of them housed in one tent. Apart from the time when the Pope visited Ireland in 1979, you probably would not have had a larger gathering of Christians in one place in this country. *Livingstone Thompson, co-author of a directory of Christian churches in Ireland.*

Devaluation
The selling of pre-signed Mass cards in retail outlets is not an acceptable practice and unfortunately some individuals and companies have exploited the traditional act of support of the church with commercial profit as its motive. These cards have no spiritual value. *Archbishop of Tuam Dr Michael Neary.*

ARTS & PARTS
Good art is obviously a subjective thing. But good art is a bit like gold—it seems to exist outside the investment market and holds its price. Artists with a reasonable reputation should still be able to sell their work in uncertain times. *Artist Robert Ballagh.*

Fool's gold
I'm being paid to make an eejit of myself and what could be better than that? *Actor Pat Shortt on his critically challenged 'Killinascully' TV series.*

Upper story
Look, you've got to realise, Gerry, people on the top floor of this place resent you and they resented me and they resent people like us. They kowtow to us but they don't like us because we are getting more money than they are. *Veteran Gay Byrne fills in Gerry Ryan on RTÉ attitudes.*

Writers' bloc
When you go outside Ireland you realise how well-regarded writers are here. The supports are there for new writers. There are routes for

them to find an audience, because writing in general is respected as part of our culture. *Playwright Paul Meade.*

Clay is the word
I think that all artists in south Monaghan feel some kind of kindred spirit with Kavanagh because he was so close to the land and wrote so eloquently—though not always positively—about the surroundings. You can't escape it, because you hear his words all the time when you see the places. *Singer, composer and former Eurovision winner Eimear Quinn on her setting of a Patrick Kavanagh poem.*

No ordinary Joe
A lady told me that for 48 years he's given her the happiest years of her life. Now that is wonderful for anyone to say—to think that my brother, that we used to consider 'just Joe', had that effect on people. *Sister Dympna at the unveiling of a statue of singer Joe Dolan in his native Mullingar.*

DE MORTUIS
Conor was one of the outstanding international diplomats, writers and historians of his generation. His clarity and depth of thought and of expression were without equal. *John Bruton, former Taoiseach and head of the EU delegation in Washington, on the death this month of Conor Cruise O'Brien.*

Ireland has lost a great Irishman and the world has lost a great citizen. *Bob McCartney, former leader of the UK Unionist Party.*

Not to have told the truth, as he saw it, to those people who didn't want to hear it was for him a betrayal of democracy. *Former Taoiseach Garret FitzGerald.*

His obvious intellect and articulacy did not prevent him being wrong on a number of issues. Some of us have not forgotten his particular vilification of John Hume and the SDLP. However, we should also remember more worthy contributions which he made to political life, journalism and UN service. *SDLP leader Mark Durkan.*

I have come to see Conor as a prophetic figure, inhabiting the somewhat lonely spaces that prophets do, on the margins. It is the nature of prophets to be prickly, awkward, angular, contrary in every sense, saying things we don't always want to hear and calling for us to change our way of thinking in building a world based on truth and justice. *Fr Patrick Claffey at the funeral mass.*

MAMMON

I don't own a shop. The Government doesn't own a shop. It's up to Tesco, it's up to Aldi, it's up to Lidl; it's up to them to cut their prices. *Tánaiste Mary Coughlan, informed that shopkeepers are looking to the Government to take responsibility for the retail crisis.*

Hot potato

I never intended to offend anyone. Holy Moses, the potato famine was in 1843 [*sic*] so what the hell is going on? I'm dumbfounded that people have taken offence, because Ireland and Australia are the two most closely aligned countries in the world. *Harvey Norman boss Gerry Harvey is accused of comparing Ireland's current economic crisis to the years of the Great Hunger.*

Alpine insularity

It promotes itself as a kind of Cayman Islands in a cold climate, and aggressively chases footloose financiers and less scrupulous British companies to move to Dublin to dodge tax. *Geographically confused Lord Oakeshott, British treasury spokesman, who also described Dublin as 'Liechtenstein on the Liffey'.*

Plane speaking

I mean it's grungy—I hate the naked aggression that you will see from Ryanair staff. I hate the filth of their aeroplanes. I think it's cheap but it's not even cheerful. But I'm an admirer of how they built up the company and how they've expanded all over Europe and so forth. *Aer Lingus chairman Colm Barrington.*

They'll all be gone. If you look at the board of Aer Lingus, with a number of notable exceptions, the rest are just like the board of bloody Fás. They're all Bertie's pals, or political appointees or trade union representatives. *Ryanair's Michael O'Leary anticipates a successful takeover of the former national airline.*

AN t-AOS ÓG

We must be sure that the next bishop of Cloyne, and every other bishop in the church, truly puts the needs of children before clergy. Otherwise the horrific pain of abuse, and the disgracing of our church by too many of its bishops, will surely continue. *Seán Ó Conaill, acting co-ordinator, Voice of the Faithful.*

I fully accept this report and all its findings and I take full responsibility for the criticism of our management of some of the issues contained in this report. We made errors, not intentionally, and I want to assure you that such errors will not be made again in this diocese. *Bishop John Magee of Cloyne on the findings on child abuse in his diocese.*

We would welcome a commitment to do it better but there are still questions about why the exact guidelines weren't implemented. *Mary Flaherty, national director, Children at Risk in Ireland.*

Bishop Magee now has to seriously consider his position and decide whether or not he can retain the confidence of the people of Cloyne in the light of these disclosures. *Seán Sherlock TD.*

I can't really look into whether or not he should be in charge of that diocese, but I have a concern in relation to his role as patron of all national schools in Cloyne and whether or not we have a role to consider in that regard. *Minister for Children Barry Andrews.*

Screening

While the internet is a fantastic resource for children to learn and develop their communication skills, adult supervision is needed. One of the most positive findings of this survey is that Irish parents are among the most likely in the EU to talk to their children about what they do online. *Martin Territt, director, European Commission Representation in Ireland.*

It is a matter of profound shame that an Education Minister of the Northern Ireland Executive stood in front of schoolchildren and lauded a terrorist hunger striker. *Stormont Assembly member Basil McCrea on Caitríona Ruane's public comments on the film* Hunger.

BANKING TURNS

I have stated on the record that many of those running our financial institutions are not and cannot be those who work with the State on where we go from here. It is a violent word but there should be a cull of executives in the banking system. *Senator Dan Boyle.*

The banks are not getting a soft, easy deal from the Government. There will not be a continuation of the current system, but root-and-branch reform which will be better for banking and better for the economy. *Minister for Communications Eamon Ryan.*

Anglo phobia
The transfer of the loans between banks did not in any way breach banking or legal regulations. However, it is clear to me, on reflection, that it was inappropriate and unacceptable from a transparency point of view. *Seán Fitzpatrick, resigning chairman, Anglo Irish Bank, on his secret transferral of an €87m loan to another bank before each year end over a period of eight years.*

We recognise and understand the sense of hurt, outrage and disappointment that people feel regarding the bank. We want to apologise unreservedly to our customers, employees, shareholders and all other stakeholders for creating this situation. *Incoming chairman Donal O'Connor.*

The bailout of Anglo Irish follows a compelling political logic. Anglo Irish funds developers, and developers fund Fianna Fáil. By any other criterion, a bailout of Anglo Irish is senseless. *UCD professor of economics Morgan Kelly.*

PARTY LINES

An Ulster Unionist-Conservative relationship which shifts Northern Ireland from the 'ledge of the union' to the very heart of the United Kingdom. That's what the Conservative Party believes in and that's what the Ulster Unionist Party believes in. *UUP leader Sir Reg Empey.*

Breakfast role

We're on a roll. The diagnosis in 2002 was that we were the porridge on the cereal shelf—it's wholesome and in certain circumstances it is a good thing to have a hot bowl of porridge. But 99 days out of 100 people would go for Crunchy Nut or whatever. Now we're transformed. I think we're going to form the next government. *Euphoric Fine Gael TD Richard Bruton.*

Class distinction

The vast majority of people have no choice but to buy their standard ticket, get on the train and go. Some people seem to think they're entitled to their newspaper and to sit in comfort when the reality is that there's no real difference between first class and economy class on the Enterprise except for the price. *MLA Thomas Burns, SDLP, South Antrim, takes exception to the predilection of Stormont civil servants for first-class travel to Dublin.*

Beeton path

Deputy Mary White is a sprout-growing expert. Mary says you have to have firm ground. If it isn't firm, they start to blow like cabbage. Her secret is very clever. In her vegetable garden she plants her sprouts where she was treading a path the year before. *Junior Minister for Food Trevor Sargent on his colleague's green credentials.*

Auto suggestion

The purpose of these changes is to incentivise consumers to purchase vehicles with lower CO_2, an important step in reducing national greenhouse gas emissions and in meeting Ireland's commitments for the purposes of the Toyota Protocol. *Kyoto driver Senator Camillus Glynn.*

HERE & THERE

We're not saying they shouldn't merge; we're just saying you've got to approach everything with extreme caution and that's the way we're going to do it. We're not going to accept that just because Alan Joyce says something in a comforting Irish brogue it must be okay. *Australian Services Union assistant secretary Linda White on a proposed merger between Qantas and British Airways, both run by Irishmen.*

Mind your language

They should have checked out the signs before putting them up but not a lot of them were wrong. You get wrongly spelt signs everywhere and Naas is the only town in Ireland where the Irish takes up more space on the sign than the English. *Anita Nic Amhlaoidh, rúnaí, Glór na Ríogh.*

We have a Polish-language clinic every week in Scariff and Ennis and it's packed out. A lot of Poles are preparing to go home. Also we have a lot of Irish looking at going abroad. *Paul Wolfe, Ennis Citizens' Information Service.*

Micilín Marbh, Co. Áth Cliath

There's no reason why we can't have bustling Gaeltacht areas in any part of Dublin, Cork, Galway or Limerick. *Éamon Ó Cuív, Minister for Gaeltacht and Community Affairs.*

Burning issue

The proposal for this incinerator dates back more than a decade to 1996. There are no effective provisions within current waste-management law or policy which would enable me to intervene directly in a PPP project which began more than a decade ago and where tenders were approved two years before I took office. *Minister for the Environment John Gormley.*

He could have used his powers as a Minister to put a stop to the incinerator. This really is his last chance to act. If he doesn't, he will be to blame if this incinerator is built. *Ruairí Quinn TD.*

John Gormley will never get in around here again after that. I'm worried about health because of course it will affect us. Traffic will get worse as there is only one road in and one road out so it has to go somewhere. *Ringsend, Dublin resident John Graham.*

Dissenting motion

There is no demand for this toilet as it is only being used about six times a day. It is money down the toilet. *Town councillor Deirdre Callaghan proposes the closure of Kilrush's unique and expensive superloo.*

Liquid assets

I think the best use that could be made of it would be the use it has already, to have a small amount of brewing kept going there. We could have it as a tourist landmark in the city. *Cork's deputy lord mayor Patricia Gosch on the future of the redundant Beamish & Crawford Brewery.*

As someone who has Guinness in my constituency and four generations of Guinness workers in my family, I am delighted to hear that the use of the pint has been extended indefinitely. Metaphorically, I'll drink to that. *MEP Gay Mitchell on the EU dero-gation on the sacrosanct imperial measure.*

Ad nausea

I see that Luas are saying that they are just replicating trams in other cities across the world. But the Luas has become a symbol of modern Dublin and I think that the people of Dublin have a justifiable sense of ownership of it. *Rathfarnham councillor John Lahar objects to external advertising on Luas trams.*

Sunstruck

I think it was extraordinary for my father when he discovered the solar alignment. When he saw the light shining through it was like he felt the cold hand of the great God Dagda, father of the Celtic Gods, touching him on the shoulder for having the temerity to come into the tomb at that time. *Eve, daughter of pioneer Newgrange arch-aeologist Michael J. Kelly.*

Shear pleasure

It was tough work and I'm a bit stiff now but it is always nice to be able to say that you're a world record holder. *Donegal man Ivan Scott after shearing 736 Romney lambs to break the strongwool lambshearing record in New Zealand.*

Trapamozzi

There is a difficulty in capturing them in Ireland for some reason and UCC are doing a survey at the moment to see what the best traps are to use. Throughout the year we were using the types they use in America and on the continent but they were useless. *Fingal Co.*

Council environmental officer George Sharpson, attempting to combat the area's mosquito infestation problem.

Cod é sin?
What we are doing, much as we do in cattle or sheep farming, is breeding the best stock we can. *Dr Richard Fitzgerald, 'Eircod' fish-farming project.*

Bell canto
We have 19 bells, which is the highest number anywhere in the world, and this is the only time of year when we get to ring them all . . . it is a wondrously beautiful note on which to end what, for many people, has been an awfully out-of-tune 2008. *Gary Maguire, bellringer, Christ Church Cathedral, Dublin, preparing to ring in the New Year.*

LISBONIANA
Ireland will get its extra wurst, but it will have to work for it. *Jan Techau, director, Alfred Oppenheimer Centre for European Policy Studies, on the retention of its commissioner.*

The message from this summit to the Irish is clear. If they vote Yes to the Lisbon Treaty, they can keep their commissioner. If they vote No, they can't. *Danish prime minister Anders Fogh Rasmussen.*

When I suggested that we should consult our Irish friends again, people said I was not being respectful of the Irish, by asking them to vote again. But we can only have the Lisbon treaty if our Irish friends vote Yes and, for that to happen, something new has to appear, and this is one commissioner per country. *French president Nicolas Sarkozy.*

The man who came to dinner
I told him what he did in Ireland on his recent State visit was an insult to the Irish people and myself personally. We don't want interference from outside about how we conduct our electoral business. It's up to the Irish people how we move forward. *Brian Crowley MEP has harsh words for Czech president Václav Klaus on his meeting with Eurosceptic Declan Ganley.*

Mé féin
For one country to stand in the way of a decision made by the parliaments of the other 26 representing almost 500 million people is not a sustainable option. The honourable course would have been to stand aside in one way or another and let the rest proceed. *Former EU commissioner Peter Sutherland.*

Plus ça change . . .
We fear, and we're very serious about this, that the EU is moving into a post-democratic phase, because we are getting back the same treaty, irrespective of declarations, irrespective of how solemn they are, irrespective of how legal they say they are. *Frank Keoghan, secretary, Gluaiseacht an Phobail.*

Runway success
I'll campaign for it [the Lisbon Treaty]. Give them free flights and they'll vote in favour. *Ryanair CEO Michael O'Leary.*

ONLY A GAME
Roy Keane hasn't been sacked because we've a bad team, he's resigning because we've a good team he feels he can't bring any further. *Sunderland football club executive Niall Quinn.*

He is a bit of a maverick and he didn't succeed on the pitch because of his pit-bull mentality. He had the outlook of a player that said, 'If you knock me down I will kick you and then we can see who is still standing at the end of the game,' and that is the way he was as a coach as well. *Per-Magnus Andersson, chairman of the Sunderland owning company.*

He is a passionate man, and I regret he leaves the job. When you are passionate, especially at the start of this career, you suffer immensely physically. Also because he is a passionate man, there is no other way for him to be in the job. When you are passionate about the game, you go out of it and then come back into it because there is no other way to be happy. That is why I believe he will be back. *Arsenal manager Arsène Wenger.*

Ladies' choice

Golf is not a need that is peculiar to persons of the male gender. *Frank Callanan SC appealing to the Supreme Court to rule that Portmarnock Golf Club is a discriminatory club under the Equal Status Act.*

Profit without honour

I don't believe that the GAA ever got the credit it deserves for opening Croke Park. Apart from keeping rugby and soccer internationals at home it has boosted the Dublin economy to the tune of millions every year but it hasn't been recognised. *Stadium director Peter McKenna.*

I was asked to pay over €400 to a GAA club rather than to a more worthy charitable organisation. I don't see why GAA clubs should be in receipt of charitable donations from the Courts Service. *Alison O'Donovan, convicted of speeding, is offered the opportunity to contribute to Sallins, Co. Kildare GAA club in lieu of a fine and penalty points.*

Moment of truth

There is no point in bullshitting the public and yourself. I believed at a point that Roy Keane was right and then I believed he was wrong. It's not about me being right. It's about giving your honest opinion to viewers and readers. *Eamon Dunphy's approach to the gentle art of sports commentating.*

CRIME & PUNISHMENT

His passion was fixing cars and bikes but his second passion was music. He was an amazing guitarist. He was into old-school rock. He had the gift of the gab too. My mother used to always say he could charm the knickers off a nun. *Family friend Darren Guilfoyle remembers Aidan O'Kane, murdered in Dublin's north inner city.*

You see them here every night, a gang of teenagers. You are afraid to say anything to them. But nothing like this has happened here before. It would make you think you wouldn't want to say anything to any of them. *East Wall resident George Turner, following O'Kane's killing.*

Bench remarks

I'm sick and tired of young people's legislation—you'd think we're driving them as slaves. It makes no sense to deprive them of a few extra euro if they want to work. What does this say to young people? Stand on street corners, scratch your backside, take drugs, but whatever you do, don't go working. *Judge John Neilan on laws preventing young people working after 10 p.m.*

While the court does not have the power to disqualify you as a councillor, I hope you act with honour and resign your seat following your conviction by a jury of your peers. *Judge Michael White to Councillor Michael 'Stroke' Fahy, found guilty of fraud.*

Demand and supply

It's always difficult to find a balance and you can never tell the media enough; you can never give them everything they want. You have to try to explain to them that we're not telling you things because we're just not. There is a reason why. And usually we try to explain that reason and our ultimate objective in any investigation is to bring the bad guys before the courts and ultimately we're not going to do anything that is going to upset that. If that means not telling the media a fact, well then that's the way it is. *Garda Kevin Donoghue, Chief Superintendent, Co. Clare, and former press officer.*

Ancestral vices

We inherited this feud. It had nothing to do with our generation. We want peace and for the fighting to stop once and for all. Generation after generation they had been getting at each other. *Christopher McCarthy, head of the Limerick McCarthy family.*

I was told today I could be whacked coming out of the hotel. I don't care if I'm shot, if I'm killed. I'll take that for the sake of my family and peace. *Jimmy Collins, head of the Collins family, following a reconciliation meeting of the warring parties.*

Life is too short and this is going on generation after generation. This is going on 15 or 20 years. I was paralysed by one of the McCarthys. I got a slap with a spade. But I can say this. The media and the Guards don't want this to stop, but we are for peace. *Jack Collopy, head of the Collopy family.*

Most of the damage in Limerick is done by young kids, four- and five-year-olds, and the system is not able to handle them. *Limerick mayor John Fitzgerald.*

The police alone are not going to resolve the problems in Limerick. It has to be a multidiscipline, collaborative approach. Prevention and intervention are more important than enforcement. *Kathleen O'Toole, head of the Garda inspectorate.*

SOCIAL & PERSONAL

Research has shown that the majority of people have never met a Traveller ... they get their images and understanding of Travellers from the media. Why, then, would 97 per cent of people not want a Traveller as a member of their family? *Ronnie Fay, director of Pavee Point Traveller organisation.*

Over the years there have been clear improvements in accommodation and education. Young Travellers have a lot more in common now with their settled peers than would have been the case in the past. Yet they know the settled community looks down on them. *Social worker Mary Rose Walker.*

We still hear arguments at every local authority about whether Travellers should have the right to travel and be nomadic. The arguments are still about why they have to travel and why they can't be better off living in houses. *Damien Peelo, director, Irish Traveller Movement.*

People from the Travelling and black communities are entitled to the same rights as anyone else and it is totally unacceptable if they are being stopped and searched purely because of the colour of their skin or their ethnic background. *Sinn Féin Policing Board member Daithí McKay.*

Post haste

Most postmen are quite good with the public; they would attempt as far as possible to gain access to the individual so that they get their mail. The unfortunate thing about this is that our workers are now under so much pressure to finish by their finishing time they cannot wait much longer than 30 seconds. They've no choice but to move on. *Bobby Weatherall, Northern Ireland branch, Communication Workers' Union.*

Where wealth accumulates . . .
On a world scale we are very rich indeed and I think that inspires many folk to be charitable for good causes at home and abroad. *Dean Houston McKelvey, Belfast's 'Black Santa'.*

. . . and men decay
As I see it, the boom was good for some but not for the rest. I think village life has been destroyed. People were content to make vast fortunes by selling land and squeezing as many houses in as possible. Now, lots of them are empty and there's no demand. I don't know what's going to happen to them. I don't know who's living here any more. *Newtownforbes, Co. Longford publican Thomas Casey.*

Late starter
It messes up my whole regime. We're used to staying at home until 11.30 p.m. and then going out. We expect to get a night out of it. You used to be able to stay out dancing until 4 a.m., a proper night out. Now you're kicked out just as you're getting going. *Penelope Martin, Co. Laois, disapproves of the early closing, under new regulations, of Dublin nightclubs.*

Short and simple annals
Our own research would say that there are about 300,000 people at consistent risk of poverty in Ireland. Eighteen per cent can't afford a holiday unless we send them on one, and one of the measures of consistent poverty—not being able to afford a meal with fish—would be far higher than what's in the European findings. *John Monaghan, national director, St Vincent de Paul.*

FINAL *WORD*
The feedback we have had to our closure has been one of devastation. One man who lost his wife would go out and sell it [*The Word*] and it was a social outlet for him. In the past, people had time like that. *Editor Sarah Macdonald laments the passing of the long-established religious magazine.*

It's a bit of a farce, really

according to Down football bainisteoir *Ross Carr: 'They impose all these new rules on the competition but deny you the chance to practise or play challenge games to get used to them.' If the* GAA *experimental rules generally meet with a mixed reception, the public attitude to the Government's handling, or mishandling, of the recession is positively negative. As for the banks . . . 'What does it say to the sponsors of the tournament?' Ross Carr continued: 'If you're putting out Mickey Mouse teams, it's two fingers up to them.' Clichés of the Month: Basically, 'Icon; iconic'. Vacancies exist for competent iconoclasts. Absolutely.*

As one of the managers who attended and co-ordinated the meetings on these issues I'm willing to give it time, but talking to spectators after yesterday's game the overriding reaction was that the physicality has been taken out of the game. 'Pussyfoot football', was how one person put it . . . *Mayo manager John O'Mahony.*

I'm very pleased with how the weekend went although I accept that it was only the first weekend. The objective was to free up games, cut out fouling and we saw that. *Liam O'Neill, chairman of the task force responsible for drawing up the new laws.*

Ould sod

If someone comes to ask me about anyone, I will tell them to 'sod off' and then they can go to chief executive Jez Moxey and he will tell them to 'sod off'. Then they can go to the owner Steve Morgan and he will tell them to 'sod off'. Then if a player comes to me and says he's unhappy, I will tell him to 'sod off'. *Wolves manager and former Republic of Ireland player and boss Mick McCarthy.*

Course of true love

I wasn't sure I was good enough to be playing in that Ryder Cup, but on the first morning Seve backed me up against a wall and spent 10 minutes telling me I was a great golfer. I remember thinking, 'Bloody hell, here is the greatest player in the world telling me I'm great. Bring it on, baby, bring it on. I was too frightened about letting Seve down not to play half-decently that week. Believe me, he is special. If I could have married him, I would have. *David Feherty, who played in the 1991 Ryder Cup.*

Home bird
I don't like sitting in a pub looking at a football match. I'd rather be standing out in the garden waiting on a pigeon. If I get one home, for me it's like how a Man United fan would feel when a striker gets a goal. *Dublin pigeon racer Robert McNally.*

RECESSIONAL
I was getting fat, dumb and happy during the good times. Now there's a leaner, more caring me for the recessionary times. We are all going to have to lose a bit of weight and work that bit harder. *Ryanair chief executive Michael O'Leary.*

Delliquescence
They just confirmed what everybody knew. They just let us work away under a cloud and denied speculation, but at the end of the day, they were pulling out from two or maybe three years ago. *Newly redundant Dell worker Denis Ryan.*

It was a very, very difficult decision given our history here, and we needed a very strong business case to make this decision. And we have. That is why it took us such a long time to make this decision. *Seán Corkery, vice-president, Dell operations in Europe.*

Poles apart
I suppose it is good news for Poland that companies are relocating from Ireland, but it would be even better if they were bringing over Irish salaries. *Sebastian Jablonski, applying for a relocated Dell job.*

We have learned a lot from Ireland, particularly the Shannon zone, and we're just doing what Ireland did. All countries fight for this kind of investment. *Marek Cieslak, president, Łódź special economic zone.*

There are many towns and villages in rural Poland where there is no pub, restaurant or hotel. Given its history, Poland has never been in a position to develop a leisure industry. But now many of the Poles who have worked in Ireland are returning to their home town to open up such establishments. *Dr Jacek Rosa, deputy head of mission, Polish embassy.*

Them and us

Unfortunately when it comes to people being hit in the pocket, it is easier to blame immigrants, so we will see a deterioration in the next year; it will become a little worse because of the economy. It is difficult to say what that will mean and what will happen because it depends on what ethnic group is asked. *Sheikh Shaheed Satardien, president, Muslim Council of Ireland.*

The problems we are faced with will require a sustained national effort in the national interest, but we are acutely aware, given our history, that the national interest has been confused with the interest of the better off. *SIPTU president Jack O'Connor.*

Crash programme

Governments have to move quickly, but it is like driving fast through fog. They are going to bump into unexpected things. But it is better to move quickly, and change policies if they don't work, than do nothing and wait to see what happens. *Economist Colm McCarthy.*

Aping their betters

Look at what they do in the US; they bring people of the highest possible business expertise to run the economy. Here, it seems if you're a buddy of the Taoiseach you get a Cabinet post. A monkey could do more than this lot are at the moment. *Jim Power, chief economist, Friends First.*

Eamon Ryan has the most experience and he was a tour operator and a bike shop owner. *Mark Fielding, Irish Small & Medium Enterprises.*

1 HP

They vandalised the whole place and wrecked the tractor. I know we are in a recession, but things must be bad when someone uses a pony as a getaway car. *Farmer Joe McGlinchey, Stranorlar, Co. Donegal, one of whose Connemara ponies was used by thieves to flee the scene of the crime.*

DE MORTUIS

It is a paradox—but one that stems from that decision in 1982—that more emphasis will be put on the short-lived Gregory Deal than on most other aspects of his political life when, in fact, Tony Gregory detested the right-wing policies of the establishment parties, including those of Fianna Fáil. *Socialist Party leader Joe Higgins. Tony Gregory died this month.*

Tony was a legend in his time. He was deeply committed to the eradication of poverty in the north inner city and much of his political life was spent asking to improve the quality of housing and education and on combating unemployment. *Labour TD Joe Costello.*

He bore his illness with remarkable courage, and never let it deflect him from his duties as a legislator and as a representative of the people in his constituency. *Labour leader Eamon Gilmore.*

So, how would he have dealt with certain politicians and their lavish tributes in the last few days? Or those people speaking profusely about him in death, but during his life when he came looking for help, never so much as put a leaflet in a letterbox? I think they would all be getting the Gregory look—you know, the sardonic one . . . *Tony Gregory's election agent Maureen O'Sullivan at his funeral mass.*

AN t-AOS ÓG

These are young people who grew up in the Celtic Tiger. They don't understand the meaning of the word recession but they are suddenly very concerned. They know they can't avoid it because it's all around them, every time they open the paper or turn on the TV. *Niall Driver, UCD careers adviser.*

All-out initiative

When our kids turn 18 we plan to show them the door and tell them there's a big world out there and they should go ahead and see it. In America I think kids are too over-protected. If they travelled a bit more there would be a lot more tolerance of other nations, countries and cultures. *Actor Liam Neeson.*

Day of atonement

The main concern here is the safeguarding of children. I have known John Magee for almost 50 years and I have always found him a reliable and dependable person. *Cardinal Brady defends the Bishop of Cloyne in the face of criticism of his handling of child abuse accusations in his diocese.*

I have called, as I've called in the past, on the priests and bishops for a new heart of atonement. We must recognise that we are all at fault to allow this horrific history of clerical child abuse to go on. We need to come out of our denial, all of us, and ensure that this never happens again. *Fr Michael Mernagh, on his 300km walk of atonement from Cobh to Dublin.*

I find that I can no longer stomach the craw-thumping, puke-inducing hypocrisy of commentators shedding crocodile tears for children who suffer from abuse and neglect, trying to blame the HSE and everybody else along the way. *Independent senator Joe O'Toole.*

SHADES OF GREEN

To be Irish once meant to be somehow rural and to have a certain cultural background. What has happened in the last 20 years is that the meaning of Irishness has become a lot more substantial. It's not just about being old-fashioned and friendly in an innocent way. Irishness still stands for a certain degree of sociability and an ability to connect easily. It stands for humour and quick-wittedness. *Gerard Tanham, Islandbridge, Co. Dublin.*

The most important thing when people choose to come here is that they want to explore the scenery, the landscape, the culture, but the thing they talk about when they leave is the people and the personalities that they have met along the way. *Simon Gregory, Tourism Ireland.*

Letter perfect

I like to think of .ie domain names as the friendly face of Ireland on the internet. It's like flying with Aer Lingus years ago, when you always got a friendly smile as you got on the plane. There are no hijacking attempts and you never get spam from a .ie address. *Daragh MacLoughlin, Letshost.ie*

Shades of black

Is Guinness not in some way an idealised version of what Ireland could have been, had nationalism proceeded in a different direction? As we enter a recession, why not imagine Ireland as Guinness in its massively moneyed heyday. It's not Catholic or Republican, but it does have a great-looking navy, resplendent in blue and cream (the Lady Patricia) and its own empire (England, Nigeria). It's an Ireland which has its aristocratic logo (a harp), is philanthropic and enjoys grouse shooting at weekends. *Laurence Keogh, creative director, McConnell's advertising agency.*

'ATIN & DRINKIN'

There are people in the restaurant world that would go to the opening of a book. Who's looking after their restaurant? They try to get ahead through the social circuit, get the face out there, mingle among the crowd and tell people to 'come to my restaurant'. I'm just not into that. *Dublin restaurateur Martin Clegg.*

Downing it

Tony said, 'Do you want to come around one evening and not have an argument about development and just talk?' So I went around and we were just sitting there, the two of us, talking about religion and music. And of course, I'm drinking. He doesn't drink very much. So I may not have noticed, but time did move on, and after a few hours Tony says, 'Um, ah, okay, it's midnight. I've got to make a phone call. Would you let yourself out?' *U2's Bono on a visit to Tony Blair, when prime minister.*

On the wagon

This is totally illegal, sometimes counterfeit alcohol which contributes to binge and under-age drinking. It is outside of regulations that are put in place to protect consumers and I would ask people not to buy from these unscrupulous sorts but from proper retail outlets. *Colin Neill, Federation of the Retail Licensed Trade, complains of the habit of some Belfast taxi drivers of selling drink from the boots of their cars.*

Rheum at the inn

Our pub culture is dying whilst our restaurant culture is thriving. The Irish have decided to choose restaurants over pubs, simply because restaurants offer us service as part of the experience, and service is a concept that is alien to so many public houses. *Food writer John McKenna.*

All wrapped up
Simple initiatives like placing all alcohol purchased in stores in the area in sealed bags can only continue to enhance the image of Temple Bar among Dubliners and all visitors to the area. *Garda Inspector Patrick Menamin.*

Uncondimentary
The pepper in Ireland doesn't smell right and someone really should do something about it. *Departing US ambassador Tom Foley's sole complaint about this country.*

FOUNDING FATHERS
The establishment of that first Dáil was completely momentous. People couldn't possibly understand what it was like for the people to have set up a parliament while the British Empire had us in full control. I think it meant everything to Daddy. To be in the Dáil was the thing. They were the most unselfish, high-minded group of people that you could imagine. *Bríd O'Doherty, daughter of Joseph O'Doherty.*

The first Dáil was so momentous that you could compare it to, say, the election of Obama. I'm thinking of rural cottages and people hearing on the radio that Ireland had its own parliament. It must have been very exciting and exhilarating for people who had got used to living under British rule. *Nora Owen, grandniece of Michael Collins.*

When I was very, very young, people would have met me who would have been through the War of Independence and who were upset about the way things worked out. They would see me and they would cry. These were people who lived in this great idealism and then were upset that things didn't work out as they should have. There was an expectation put onto me by some that I would do something amazing to unite Ireland. I was five! *Professor Cathal Brugha, grandson of Cathal Brugha and Terence MacSwiney.*

He was always incredibly respectful and honoured to be a member of the Dáil—I suppose because they literally fought for it. We were always brought up with the thought that the Dáil wasn't something that was always there. Because of where they came from, they saw that just getting independence was not an end in itself, that we needed economic independence as well. *Eoin Ryan MEP, grandson of James Ryan.*

PARTY LINES
Just as people understandably ask why oil and gas price reductions have not been fully passed on to customers, many are also wondering are they getting the full benefits of devolution. *SDLP leader Mark Durkan.*

Party lions
What I don't like is this idea that it is the Taoiseach, the Minister for Finance and myself running the show. It has been portrayed that way and I don't like it. *Tánaiste Mary Coughlan.*

It's my intention to remain as long as the party finds me useful. I am the party president, but I am not vainglorious about it. I'm not precious about it. I am very much part of a collective leadership. *Sinn Féin president Gerry Adams.*

I still find it very difficult when I see Ian to think about him in any terms other than as my leader. *NI First Minister and DUP leader Peter Robinson.*

I suggested in the suggestion box that Paisley should be Pope. *Ian Junior on the family holiday visit to the Vatican.*

I used to have rows with Bertie Ahern and it was very hard to have rows with him. No matter what you said, it was just absorbed into the features and that was the end of it. It went nowhere. *Fine Gael leader Enda Kenny.*

I'd prefer to be arm-wrestling with Cowen rather than having to constantly dance around Bertie. *Labour leader Eamon Gilmore.*

I have no problem with democratic accountability, but as long as I am running this Government I will run it as I see fit and as I believe, based on my philosophy. *Taoiseach Brian Cowen.*

Emergency exit

I am the most junior of the junior ministers. I am the last. I am obviously prepared to place my office at the disposal of the Taoiseach if the decision was to reduce. I would go without fuss or protest. *Martin Mansergh, minister of state for the OPW.*

Would the world end if there was a minister or two less? We have to keep our eye on the big picture. *Junior minister Noel Ahern.*

LAW & ORDER

I never saw anyone move so fast. He was moving like a leprechaun. *Sergeant Vincent Muldoon, Lettermacaward, Co. Donegal, in evidence on a driver banned for exceeding the speed limit.*

Cois tine

I was disappointed to note that over the Christmas period An Garda Síochána had to investigate a number of murders. I can't have a Garda member sitting in every living room in the country. *Garda Commissioner Fachtna Murphy on domestic violence.*

Mixed dozen

Effectively, you end up with a jury which very often consists solely of people who are very young or not employed and that is not a balanced thing. There should, of course, be some of those people on the jury but they shouldn't all be from these categories. *DPP James Hamilton.*

I've made my decision. If he doesn't like it he can lump it or go to a higher court. This man lectures this country . . . He should be seen and not heard. *District Court Judge Seán McBride criticises the DPP for insisting he should hear a case which the judge felt should have been sent to the Circuit Court.*

Droit de seigneur

Has the female half of the population to accept that one or more of them might be targets because of a rapist's constitutional rights? *Mr Justice Paul Carney.*

WAR & PEACE

Last year I had 28 different meetings with officials from the department or the HSE. And while all the officials I've dealt with have been very cordial and welcoming, the end result is that, going into 2009, I don't know what my budget will be for this service for the most vulnerable people you could possibly imagine. *Fr Michael Begley, director, Irish Centre for the Care of Survivors of Torture.*

Joined-up thinking

Here was what Thomas Kettle would memorably describe, less than a decade later, as 'the secret scripture of the poor' that would drive tens of thousands of young Irish men into the British army to sacrifice their lives so that their families could eat. *President Mary McAleese on the endemic poverty of the early twentieth century.*

There is a whole host of reasons why young Irishmen joined the army in the early part of the twentieth century and it is wrong to try and rewrite history by suggesting it was poverty alone, or substantially, that was the main factor. People willingly joined the British army to fight for what was their country at the time and to serve the crown. *DUP junior minister Jeffrey Donaldson.*

Pieces of silver

These people told us how hurt they were that no one in authority ever recognised or marked their loss. They will never stand up in a public meeting. They will never stand in front of a camera or microphone and say that they agree with this recommendation. Nor should they have to. They fear it may sound like they are putting a monetary value on their loved one. *Lord Eames on the Commission proposal to compensate the families of victims of the Troubles to the tune of £12,000 per victim.*

My family will be put in the same category as IRA scum who murdered my parents. I for one will not accept a penny of this blood money. *Michelle Williams, whose parents were victims of the 1993 Shankill Road bombing.*

Fourthreich opinion

It's particularly appalling to suggest that a member of this House conducts himself in a manner that resembles the conduct of the chief propagandist of Hitler's Nazi Party, and quite extraordinary that such remarks should be made by a Sinn Féin member about the only Jewish member of this parliament. *Alan Shatter TD responds to Aengus Ó Snodaigh's comparing him to Dr Goebbels for his comments on the Gaza incursion.*

I may need another ambassador here in addition to me to educate the Irish people about Jewish history . . . about what the state of Israel is about. *Israeli ambassador Dr Evrony.*

ARTS & PARTS

I had such a good time making those two movies, too much of a good time on *Ella Enchanted.* I had never encountered a place that was so much fun as Dublin and with such permissive social habits. By the time *Becoming Jane* came around, I was much more in control. *Actress Anne Hathaway.*

Escape roots

What's there not to enjoy? When we had nothing, all we had was our music, our culture; it has always been a shining light through the dark times of the past. We still have our roots, our culture, our music, and I have no doubt it will continue to sustain and entertain us through whatever life throws at us. *Actor Stephen Rea.*

No-no logo

I have to say this is extremely inappropriate to either the BBC or Northern Ireland, or identity design in general. This is almost like a really bad joke. It's like the Batman logo on acid and poorly executed. The biggest problem I see is that it looks like a very aggressive logo, with its pointy edges and hazardous colour. *Armin Vit, principal of New York design consultancy UnderConsideration, on the new BBC Northern Ireland logo—a green stylised 'N' plus a dot representing 'I'.*

Winner all right

The feeling of many of the judges with *The Secret Scripture* was that there was a lot wrong with it and it was flawed in many ways. Almost nobody liked the ending . . . *Novelist Sebastian Barry, winner of the Costa book award for* The Secret Scripture.

Crocodile tears
My instinct at the time was to stay quiet and shut up and let whatever was going to happen happen. It was an extraordinary moment: the Taoiseach was about to cry on national television. *RTÉ newsreader Bryan Dobson on his 2006 interview with Bertie Ahern.*

Dying fall
I was devastated that this gorgeous creature, Violetta, had sacrificed herself for love and had died in the end. But I also remember that the soprano was enormous because when she was about to collapse there was this tiny tenor opposite her and I thought she was going to flatten him. *Verdi's* La Traviata *as experienced by eleven-year-old Majella Cullagh who was subsequently to play the same lead role at Glyndebourne.*

Foot in the door
I'm getting myself into that house if it's the last thing I do. I'm getting out of this recession. That's my motto. You have to razzle-dazzle on a day like this. We need to look fabulous and that's what I'm doing. *Drag queen Davina Devine, auditioning in Dublin for the Big Brother reality TV series.*

HERE & THERE
I love being here with my children. But I have a kind of love-hate relationship with Ireland. I'd love to be able to think I could live here, but my head won't let me. I can't reconcile things that have happened. There's a certain sadness about my childhood and a sadness about Ireland. The poverty. The sickness. I suppose, the hardship. *London-based millionaire businessman Vince Power.*

Hole that tiger!
We are responsible for the deaths of four Tasmanian tigers. We can prove at least one of these was shot at the request of the then museum director in 1917, which is now stuffed and sitting in the National History Museum. *Museum director Nigel Monaghan on the sad fate of* Thylacinus cynocephalus, *believed to be extinct since 1936.*

Doing the dirt

I find it very frustrating when they just come to a town for a day here or there because these things cast a shadow on an area for a long time. They have to realise the damage these surveys can do. *John Mulvihill, mayor of Cobh, judged to be the dirtiest town in Ireland.*

Beer and skittles

I love the sunshine and the laid-back lifestyle so I really don't mind what I do. It's surprising how you can tolerate a job in office administration over here. At work, they bring beer and wine around on Fridays. One afternoon I was working in the reception of a company and was made to play cricket in the afternoon. *Emigrant Jenny O'Grady approves of Australia.*

In for a penny

We went to the Bank of Ireland, in Dublin, were sent to an office and had an account opened within minutes. I once went to a well-known bank in Paris and they told me that they couldn't open an account for a numismatic company. When I asked them why, they said they didn't know the numismatic business very well . . . *Numismatist Jérôme Lacroix, now based in Ireland.*

Offaly offensive

If I was from Offaly I'd be complaining every day of the week. The county's in an awful state. I heard that the storms were very bad in Tullamore after Christmas and caused up to €10m worth of improvements to the town. *Satirist Oliver Callan of Nob Nation.*

SOCIAL & PERSONAL

I never knew anyone who had a three-grand handbag. Certainly, most people did better than they had done in the 1980s, but there was an incredible lack of willingness to end the divisive inequalities that have always existed in Ireland. *Writer Joseph O'Connor.*

Stooping to conquer

I am never too proud to pick a penny up from the floor. I grew up with nothing and I know the value of money. *Developer Seán Dunne, who paid €380m for a Ballsbridge, Dublin site.*

We need €100,000, and we don't have anything like that. We were hoping maybe that Seán Dunne would be able to help us out because he said he was basing his Ballsbridge building on our dome, but now maybe isn't the best time to go after him. *Dr John McCrodden, hon. treasurer, St Stephen's (Peppercanister) Church, Dublin, the dome of which is in serious need of restoration.*

Mosaic law
The mosaic of a new Ireland which we are challenged to create must be one where the dignity of each person is recognised for what it is. That is why we welcome everyone who comes to our shores for the dignity that belongs to them. *Archbishop of Dublin Diarmuid Martin.*

Tit and polish
If you want to do a blow job, I pay an extra tenner, so that would be £25. Sex, an extra tenner. You do a bit of cleaning for an hour, then a bit of fun at the end of it. *Belfast's 'Marty' (surname withheld) details his tariff for nude cleaning services.*

ACUTE ANGLO
Seán Fitzpatrick deceived, when he was chief executive and chairman, his board, shareholders, general public and staff. *Joe Meade, financial services ombudsman, on the secret loans to the former chairman of Anglo Irish Bank, subsequently nationalised.*

Once upon a time, not very long ago, in this country we had a man called 'Ansbacher man'. 'Ansbacher man' seems to have had a son called 'Anglo man' and the principal and first son of 'Anglo man' is Mr Seánie Fitzpatrick. *Labour finance spokeswoman Joan Burton.*

You were blindfolded, you were sitting on your hands, you had your mouth gagged and you had your ears covered. *Fianna Fáil Senator Geraldine Feeney disapproves of the inaction of the financial regulator.*

Fellow shareholders, in case you didn't know, the patient is dead. 'Twas announced last night by the minister. This is the wake. Now the reading of the will comes later, when the assessor announces how much we will get. *Shareholder Donal O'Callaghan at the EGM of the failed Anglo Irish Bank.*

I think the auditors were supposed to have done an audit on the whole thing and missed this parcel of €84m floating in and out like a tennis ball. Nobody raised the possibility of Ernst & Young handing back their fee; that might be a nice move for everybody. *Veteran broadcaster Gay Byrne at the* EGM.

I was never in the tent at the Galway races and never visited the Galway races, nor did I receive representations from developers or bankers about this particular financial institution. *Finance minister Brian Lenihan.*

The chickens in the Galway tent are now firmly coming home to roost. *Sinn Féin* TD *Arthur Morgan.*

CÚPLA FOCAL

If the Government believes that by 2028 one in 20 will be speaking Irish every day, we should have no problem getting one in 20 UCD students speaking Irish for a week. *Students' union president Aodhán Ó Deá on the college's 'No Béarla' promotion.*

We believe that the ability to use predictive text in Irish without needing to acquire new technology will have an immensely positive effect on the usage of the language, particularly amongst young people in education, for whom SMS is a primary means of communication. *Carolan Lennon, consumer director, Vodafone Ireland.*

Honourable takeaway

I focus on what's known as *pin yin* or phonetic Chinese. We do basic greetings and language to get around. We also teach students how to order food. *Xiao Dong Li, who teaches Chinese to the girls of Loreto, Bray.*

Well bread

You can't just go into a shop and ask in English for a sliced pan and a copy of *Paris Turf*. If you do stuff like that they will ignore you and they can be arrogant. But if you say '*Bonjour*' and are polite, and make an effort, they are great. *France-based Co. Kildare jockey Dean Gallagher on* la vie Parisienne.

Generation game

Some of the senior matches, it's ridiculous the stuff that's shouted in. Like, I'm no prude, I can do bad language myself. But I think some of it is really, really vindictive. It's not even to do with how you're playing, but to do with who you are and who your family are, and your ancestors were. *Former Antrim hurler Olcan McFetridge.*

LOST WORD

They are probably the most drastic decisions any government in the last 30 or 40 decades has had to make. *Minister Dermot Ahern remembers 1690.*

February 2009

Our advice to motorists is to stay off the roads

warns Sergeant Jim Kelly of Naas Garda, Co. Kildare. It is almost a real winter for once, and the Sergeant goes on to complain that 'young fellas are opening car doors and throwing snowballs at the drivers, which can cause accidents'. Somewhat confusingly, it is the driest February for 23 years, with Birr, Co. Offaly, recording the lowest rainfall at 15.6mm. Does snow count? For the average punter, young fellas excepted, the snow seems only to heighten the gloom and doom of the omnipresent recession. Cliché of the Month courtesy of the Tánaiste, Mary Coughlan, for whom it is important to say, 'it is important to say' seriatim.

I think the biggest challenge really was coping with the different fluctuations in temperature. Starting out in the Antarctic it was as low as -20°, and later that day, in Cape Town, it was 28°. *Ian Donovan, first man to run marathons on all seven continents in less than seven days.*

I did feel that my blindness was putting a lot more pressure on my teammates, as I couldn't put up the tent. Well, I could, but I was very slow. I would crawl in and get the sleeping mats out, blow up the thermorests and organise the sleeping bags, but after that I was very reliant on them. *Mark Pollock, Hollywood, Co. Down, the first blind man to reach the South Pole.*

Deep and crisp ... and even snow
This winter we have had quite a few nights with sharp frost and it's been a while since the Dublin region has had such significant falls of snow. It's unusual in that sense, but on the other hand it's winter weather. *Gerry Murphy, Met Éireann.*

ARTS & PARTS

It's time to bring the '80s back to Dublin. The Irish understand me better than any audience in the world. And I should know; for instance, I've toured Australia 18 times. *Veteran jazzman Acker Bilk.*

Cyrillic character

He was a very difficult man. This is only my experience and I do think I had it a bit easier, but he kind of dominated a room. There'd be an atmosphere. I don't know if he meant to, but he just did . . . As he had grown older and become more established, the world started to revolve around him. But also it was a generation thing. He was a man when men were the centre of everything, the centre of family. I think he was a fantastic actor, a ground-breaking actor. *Actress daughter Catherine on her father, Cyril Cusack.*

Out for the Count

In all the years that I have lived with this exceptional portrait by the great Sir William Orpen I have never ceased to be fascinated and amazed at the way that the artist captured the essence of my grandfather—the singer, the man, the father, and the husband. It is now time for this work to give friendship and pleasure to a new home. *John Count McCormack's grandson decides to sell.*

Ticking off

There's nothing really annoying about them, but they do have this habit of working right up to the very last second. On *War*, the very last song we did was *40*. The studio clock was ticking and the next band due in were waiting outside the door. It happened again on this album—it happens on every U2 album. *Producer Steve Lillywhite.*

Rural electrification

We all want to be uplifted. The extent of the bad news is one of the reasons that newspaper sales are declining. It is lovely to be able to lift one's mood from time to time by tuning into a country music channel. *Senator Donie Cassidy.*

Levelling the score

I met Spike when he came to see his daughter Jane in a show we were in together, for which I was the Musical Director. 'Who wrote that bloody awful music?' was Spike's opening line. *Paul Boyd and colleague, acting in the Hawk's Well Theatre adaptation of Spike Milligan's novel* Puckoon.

Return empty
I vowed not to go back to Waterford. I have played to half-filled halls in other parts of the world. But in your own home town? *Entertainer Gilbert O'Sullivan.*

Downward aspiral
What they used to roar at me, and what the origin of it is I'm not too certain, was 'Get them off ya, Maggie!' As crude as it gets. All you could do was laugh and walk on, because it wasn't actually intended as a kind of sexist remark. *Biddy White Lennon, who played Maggie in the RTÉ series 'The Riordans', first screened in 1965.*

Jaunting car
This is Beckett's car—an old Citroën—which he had from 1963 to 1989—and that fascinates me in a sense. You read about the car; it's well documented. One well-known celebrity was driven around Paris in it and said that it was only through divine intervention that Beckett didn't get him killed. *Photographer John Minihan explains a picture in an exhibition of his work.*

Shy look
He is shy; most photographers are. Having a camera allows us to really look at people, and he is a master of more than one craft. He has a great eye and great taste. What he is best at is getting the best out of people. *Photographer and movie director Conor Horgan on fellow photographer Tony Higgins.*

FAITH & MORALS
Every day there are new revelations from the banks; same from the church. What people want most of all now is honesty. It needs us to return to God and the basic messages of the Gospel values, but above all, it needs those in authority to listen to and support a mobilised grassroots. *Fr Harry Bohan.*

It is a grave concern that our nation's financial crisis is rapidly becoming a profound social crisis. For many people it has been a shattering experience at a deeply personal level. There is now a collective sense of grief, fear, anger but also a kind of reawakening. *Most Rev. Jim Moriarty, Bishop of Kildare & Leighlin.*

Jesus shaves

Lent is quite properly a penitential season. But that doesn't mean we can't have some fun with it while doing good for others. Shaving one's head is a traditional way of doing penance. Doing it with a bunch of friends in front of your colleagues and teachers is a bit of a laugh. And doing it for a worthy cause is the best of both worlds. *Patrick Burke, Church of Ireland Theological Institute.*

WE SPORTED & PLAYED

My dad has no interest in football. He used to come and see me play when I was six or seven but he hasn't got a clue. He still thinks I am a centre forward or something. *Dubliner Willie Flood, having joined Celtic.*

Kick startle

I could believe the push and shove. But that action of kicking is not on. You looked around and there were a lot of jaws open to say: 'Did that really happen?' *Carlton Aussie Rules coach Brett Ratten on an assault on fellow player Cameron Cloke by Setanta Ó hAilpín.*

It's completely out of character for him. Normally he's one of the nicest blokes you'll ever meet and one of the most dedicated blokes at training. I think all of the blokes at our club would definitely welcome him and would be excited to help him get back on his horse again. *David Teague, Northern Bullivants VFL club.*

Track record

It's not something I'm going to play down—I am ecstatic. All 3,000 winners have taken a lot of hard work. I feel very privileged to have ridden 3,000 winners when the jockeys who came before me, who were as good or better than me, didn't ride as many. *Moneynick, Co. Antrim jockey Tony McCoy.*

Mexican waiver

Alex Ferguson, my old manager, comes out and says, 'You never know what he is going to do next.' What did he think I was going to do? Go backpacking around Mexico? I have five kids. Football is in my blood! I'd just had enough at Sunderland. Things had changed. End of bloody story. *Roy Keane explains.*

DE MORTUIS

As a playwright, journalist and radio contributor, Hugh infused his work with a unique wit, all the while demonstrating a great intuition, perceptiveness and forgiveness of human nature. *President Mary McAleese. Hugh Leonard, aka Jack Keyes-Byrne, died this month.*

A true giant of Irish theatre, who wrote some of the most popular and enduring plays of the twentieth century. *Arts Council director Mary Cloake.*

He was interested in all sorts of things. He was magnificent on the subject of old films and positively encyclopaedic on the canals of France. And though his observations were tough and often hurtful, he has said some of the funniest lines I've ever heard. He once said, of an American PR woman, that 'she never had an unspoken thought in her life'. *Gate Theatre director Michael Colgan.*

Allez, allez, go, Jack, sail on and enjoy the Kingdom of Heaven. *Monsignor Paddy Finn at the funeral Mass.*

Ave atque vale

He loved being surrounded by a party, good friends, family and fine wine. At yesterday's wake he would have been delighted to know that, true to his passion for a good party, he was the first to arrive and the last to leave! *Ross Glacken on his father, Brendan, former* Irish Times *humorous columnist.*

Rites issues

People don't die between nine and five, so we have to put a service out there to cater for the public 24/7 as well. We're dealing with people who are newly bereaved. How delicate a customer can you deal with? It's majorly important that we have the best type of service available to them. *Melvyn Colville, Glasnevin Cemeteries Group.*

Not everybody is cut out for this job. Personality is the big thing. You have to be able to show compassion towards people who are dealing with loss. Some people think there is a taboo attached to dealing with the dead and would be afraid to be involved in our business. When I tell people what I do for a living, the odd time they are a bit unnerved by it but then a lot of people find it interesting and they start to ask you questions. Death can be very interesting to some people. *Bray, Co. Wicklow undertaker Philip Ward.*

BRICKS & MORTAR

At the oral appeal a lot of people and some of the residents referred to themselves as 'people of means'. So I think there is a snobbish element with Ballsbridge about Ballsbridge. I actually live in Ballsbridge; it is full of very nice people but there is an element of people who think that they speak for Ireland when they speak for Ballsbridge. *Property developer Seán Dunne, whose proposed €1.5 billion scheme was refused planning permission.*

He really has a cheek. That's all wrong. That's a no-no. It's not true. It's a nice friendly area. I don't think there's anything snobbish about it. I suppose he had to say something. *Clyde Road, Ballsbridge resident Amelda Burke.*

Soft cell
The gaol has been lying empty for twenty-two years and the future of this historic building looked bleak. Very soon this city, which is the oldest in Ireland, will have one of the most unusual hotels in Europe. *Armagh Mayor Noel Sheridan.*

Danger zoning
I was intimidated and got phone calls at all hours threatening to dismantle my election campaign. I got one call late at night warning me that they would tear me to shreds. This is nothing short of bullying and coercion and it is disgraceful. *Clare Co. Councillor Cathal Crowe, assailed by a development company seeking land rezoning.*

Bad manors
Developers are behaving like feudal lords. The odds are stacked against the owner. The people occupying are having to pay for the

whole complex. *Evelyn Hanlon, Dublin City Council housing division, on the withholding of property management fees for unsold units.*

Name your price. It's a phrase I'm hearing over and over from the owners of our properties. During the good times, you would never hear it. It's still fairly rare among the old monied set who have had a country pile in the family for generations. But the nouveau riche yuppies who bought fabulous mansions in the 1990s, businessmen who are finding the going very rough now, are open to any offer. *John Coakley, Adams & Butler luxury advisory service.*

SHADES OF GREEN
What interests me particularly about his play—and maybe there's a bit of personal thesis here—is the notion of what constitutes 'Irishness'. One of the problems that comes up time and time again seems to be this notion of being 'pure' Irish. If you are Protestant, born in the Northern part of the island and deeply into the Protestant tradition, that somehow does not make you a legitimate Irish person. *Actor Ian McIlhenny in a new production of Brian Friel's* Home Place.

Turfed out
I don't think being Irish has played a huge part in my success. Being foreign in New York is not exactly a big deal. I have to play down my Irish accent on TV. You can't come across as a big bogger because people won't understand you. *TV presenter Emma Buckley.*

American dream
They have a very romantic view of Ireland there [Hollywood], a very Emerald Isle view . . . no idea what has been happening in modern times. Or if you talked to them about the Troubles—you might as well be talking about Lebanon. No understanding, and they didn't really want to understand, either. But being Irish there marks you out as being a kind of curiosity. And it gives you, in a weird way, a kind of an identity as an outsider. And Hollywood is just made up of outsiders. *Actor Gabriel Byrne.*

Sea of Persia
I was very pleasantly surprised to find that the Emirates are very similar to the Irish in the predisposition to be friendly and the use of

small talk to start a conversation. One of the surprising things is the fact that they don't particularly like to say 'no'. It took me a while to understand that the lack of an answer to a particular question can often be as close as you'll get to hearing a negative response. *John Daly, Abu Dhabi Securities Exchange.*

MAMMON

I had to sit through a function recently where I was subjected to a lecture from a tax exile on how to do our business and where we should be spending our hard-earned money. The whole scheme is a source of great annoyance to those who have no choice—their taxes are stopped from their salaries automatically as well as other levies. *Bernard Allen, chairman, Public Accounts Committee.*

Mountebankers

My total disclosed compensation in the report on accounts, I think, was €2.9m . . . [this year] it will be less than €2m. *Outgoing Bank of Ireland chief Brian Goggin.*

In the name of God, what kind of alternative planet are these guys living on? *Former Labour leader Pat Rabbitte TD.*

A group of clowns who have disgraced themselves over many years who had one aim in the negotiations—the saving of their jobs. *Senator Shane Ross.*

I can't say when the fraud squad will go in. I know there are people who want to see people clamped in irons. *Justice minister Dermot Ahern.*

In the United States you see people who are white-collar criminals led out in handcuffs. I want to see the same regime in this country, and I believe we will get the same regime in this country. *Minister for the Environment John Gormley.*

There are some of our members who dread going out in public as in small towns and the like. They get attacked by the locals who think they are all on big bonuses and great salaries. *Larry Broderick, general secretary, Irish Bank Officials Association.*

Market value

The dynamic of a market, where the stallholders sell what they produce direct to shoppers, is very special. It creates a buzz, and energy and a business stimulant that is just brilliant, particularly within a city centre. Our plans are to facilitate this 'buzz' by providing a more perfect environment for both the stallholders and the shoppers. *David O'Mahony, Limerick Market Trustees.*

Nappy medium

This is not about politics; it is about economics and those who are in charge of economics. This is all about bringing the benefit of two economies on the one island together and making the most of it. How can you be a Scrooge and blame people from the south . . . for buying, for example, Pampers at half price in Newry? *Gerard O'Hare, chairman, Parker Green International.*

A LITTLE LEARNING

We need to face the unpalatable fact that many students entering courses in science and technology are not able to handle the cognitive demands of these courses and will either drop out or struggle through to get poor degrees. The knowledge economy will not be built on these students. *Dr Peter Childs, University of Limerick.*

Shaggy dog's story

They read to Setanta. It builds their confidence. They are reading to the dog so they concentrate on the dog rather than the words or the teacher. It enables social interaction and relaxes them; reading to the dog helps to keep them relaxed. The dog places no demands on them. *Denise Chambers, resource teacher, Sallins NS, Co. Kildare.*

Role call

One thing that was hammered home in Clongowes was that even to the younger boys in the school you're a role model. There's a natural continuum of that in the world of sport, the game I'm in now. We're very aware that if we act the mick then it's going to make the papers, but that if we set a good example that might make the papers too. *Rugby international Gordon D'Arcy.*

Closed Peig

The new generation of young people don't have the same negative associations with Irish as some older people have. They're the first generation who's grown up with an Irish-language TV station like TG4 which has the same kind of shows, music, chat-shows, soaps and documentaries as any other channel, except they're Irish. *New Yorker and* nua-ghaeilgeoir *Des Bishop.*

Glad hand

I have found this role to be both enriching and fulfilling. Above all—a point brought home to me when I shake the hands of tomorrow's leaders as they cross the stage at graduation—it has been an honour and a privilege. *Retiring Queen's University chancellor George Mitchell.*

Mother-of-purl

I'm trying to promote knitting so that people will pick it up again. I've tried knitting with telephone poles at an exhibition once—it was fantastic and great fun. It's my therapy and I have spoken to so many people who say it relaxes them. *Co. Kildare knitting enthusiast Eva Kavanagh.*

RECESSIONAL

Like alcoholics on a binge, we need to reach rock bottom. We need a reality check before we can rebuild. *Independent senator Eoghan Harris.*

Infirm of purrrpose

I don't think the regulator could have eyeballed the office cat in the banks! *Labour finance spokeswoman Joan Burton.*

Chase to the cut

It's not for individuals to say, 'I'm taking a cut,' or 'I'm not taking a cut.' It's for the organisation to decide and then we all row in. *Broadcaster George Hook on broadcaster Eamon Dunphy's voluntary 10 per cent.*

If I were being paid by the State I would take a pay cut but I'm not. If you are being paid by the State, you are obviously adding to the deficit. If you are paid by someone else and you pay taxes, your pay is detracting from that deficit. So let's analyse it properly. *Economic commentator David McWilliams.*

Stepping up to the plates
I didn't believe in writing a script or looking down for the evening. I want to look at everyone in the eye and say a few things. *Taoiseach Brian Cowen at the Dublin Chamber of Commerce dinner.*

A person beside me said, 'Where has this speech been for that last six months?' It was of such importance. *Chamber diner and EPS Consulting managing director Peter Brennan.*

Making speeches is not enough in the current climate. Making good speeches is not enough. You've got to be seen to be taking action. *Michael Keane, Insight Consultants.*

Troops out
It is only radical thinking like abolishing the Army that will ensure we get out of this financial crisis with the minimum of hardship for ordinary people. *Paddy Kenneally, Republican Sinn Féin spokesman, Co. Clare.*

HERE & THERE
It's very important to have one name because it's a question of identity and credibility. People say to me as a public representative: 'How can the council be looking after our basic needs if they can't even get our name right?' *South Dublin councillor Gus O'Connell, whose bailiwick encompasses Palmerstown . . . or Palmerston.*

Sex Nations
I'll put it this way: you see fellas going to Edinburgh and Cardiff and it's like six lads heading off on a stag. You'll meet them the last day in the airport and they're all looking a bit sheepish and bedraggled. Probably the same clothes they were in at the match. Then you meet the same guys in Rome. They've all got their wives with them. They're really well dressed. They've had a lovely, civilised weekend, nice wine, nice food. Their partners say to them, 'You can go on your own to Scotland and Wales, but I'm coming to Rome.' *Former rugby international Denis Hickie.*

C-change

The situation in the euro-area countries would be much worse and much more difficult if we didn't have the euro. I always mention the case of Ireland, comparing it to Iceland, so this is indeed a great demonstration of the success of the euro area. *European Commission president José Mañuel Barroso.*

Close-run think

It never had an awful lot. It never demanded an awful lot—frustratingly easygoing, almost philosophical people . . . But the almost philosophical people of Leitrim are now very, very angry because of the Government's move to split our beautiful little county of 28,000 into two constituencies. *Manorhamilton councillor Micheál Colreavy.*

Big Bang

It was very exciting. We have a lot of people around because of the mid-term break, so when the Gardaí were here stopping traffic, everybody wanted to know what was going on. Then the army arrived with guns and everything, so we were all outside watching the controlled explosion from behind the wall. It was great. *Ann Waters, manager, Hook Head lighthouse, at the discovery of an old warning detonator device.*

Ticket-of-leave

In a few days' time I'm leaving and I won't be back, and I'll just be some Irish person that grew up here and doesn't exist any more. When you have no choice, you have no choice. We can't afford to rent anywhere; we can't afford to buy anywhere. It's a no-brainer. It's just two words: 'No money' . . . So I bought a one-way ticket. *Samantha Melia heads for Perth, Australia.*

The difficulty is that today, there's nowhere to go. Even Australia seems to be going downhill. I heard of an Irish architect who sent an email home saying he got the last job in Brisbane. *John Graby, rector, Royal Institute of Architects of Ireland.*

I left Dublin nine years ago when the Celtic Tiger was starting. I obviously knew I wasn't cut out to be rich. *Fashion designer Paul Costelloe, London.*

SOCIAL & PERSONAL

I ain't running. I wouldn't be able to lie, I'm afraid. I swear to God I don't want to run for office. I'm not a politician—I'm the opposite of what a politician should be. *Presenter and commentator Eamon Dunphy refuses to have greatness thrust upon him.*

Apposite sex

I believe it does make a difference if there are very few women in politics and finance. There's been a lot of talk about a testosterone-driven, unregulated culture where people are rewarded for short-term gains. Perhaps this would be less likely to happen if women were in positions of authority. *Senator Ivana Bacik.*

Didn't you know that women run the show? Women are in charge. It is only that we men, we think we are running the show. They tell a story about a woman saying, 'Ahh, the virgin birth, that I can believe— but three wise men, impossible.' *Archbishop Desmond Tutu on a Dublin visit.*

Loan Arranger

I was 16, Adam was 17. We were stuck out in Malahide without any bus fare. Adam says: 'I know, let's get a bank loan. That's what banks are for.' We went down to the Northern Bank in Malahide, but it was lunch hour and it was closed. Adam climbed up the railings and started knocking on the window of the bank. The manager came to the window with a sandwich in his mouth. I saw the door opening and Adam going in. A few minutes later he re-emerged and had managed to get a bank loan of £2. *The Edge, U2's guitarist.*

Bored minutes

Over the past three years, February 27 has been the day most stricken by absence as boredom starts to creep into the workplace. With Christmas well and truly over and the Easter holidays over a month away, employees don't feel they have anything to look forward to, so take the opportunity to take an extra holiday. *Alan Price, Peninsula Ireland employment law consultancy.*

Inis dom
I have a registrar here at the moment and she can't believe the knowledge that I have about patients. There is a sort of unspoken communal knowledge here that is very bizarre. That said, you have to remain slightly removed from it as a professional. I don't believe that going totally native helps anyone. *Dr Kevin Quinn, Árainn Mhór, off the Donegal coast.*

Bar code
Psychology comes in very handy when you work in a bar. A lot of the people you meet are lunatics, so that kind of background is very helpful. *Mark Flanagan, Belfast-born Los Angeles bar owner and former psychology student.*

Felo de se
Unemployment and fear of unemployment has certainly been a recurring theme in petitions. There also seems to be an increase in prayers for people affected by suicide. I think we need to focus on a message of hope. *Fr Michael Cusack, novena director, Galway cathedral.*

The indications are that maybe one-third—at least—of single-vehicle road accidents may be hidden cases of suicide, but they are currently all regarded as accidents. Recent figures over the last year show an increase in accidental poisoning by paracetamol, which is a very common method of self-harm, and we are also looking into that area. *Dr Ella Arensman, National Suicide Research Foundation.*

PARTY LINES
Nothing to the nationalist community, nothing to the unionist community, nothing to the Irish Republic and nothing to the well-being of Northern Ireland. One must ask the question—why under the living sun should it survive? *The DUP's Lord Morrow disapproves of the North/South Ministerial Council.*

Grin and bare it
We are lying there bollix naked next to Fianna Fáil. We have been screwed by them a few times, but we are hoping we can roll them around to get what we want over the longer term. *Green Party TD Paul Gogarty.*

Criminal conversation

While they may be covered legally in some circumstances against action, they are not covered in parliamentary procedure. Where members make direct allegations of a criminal behaviour against other members when there have been no convictions, I will rule such allegations as unparliamentary. *Assembly Speaker William Hay, following comments by DUP's Nelson McCausland on Gerry Adams.*

LESSER BREEDS

Our detection dogs are a key element of the Customs enforcement effort. Since the inception of our canine programme in 2001 they have helped us to intercept vast quantities of drugs, cigarettes and currency. We also know that their very presence acts as a deterrent for potential smugglers. *Maria Ryan, manager, Revenue's dog unit.*

Ferry fur fetched?

The Irish badgers are Spanish, but the British badgers are not. The fauna of Ireland seems to be divergent. How does one explain this? It seems to me that most animals in Ireland came by boat. *Professor Dan Bradley, TCD.*

Deer departed

We are a conservative organisation. We are not a deer-shooting organisation, but deer have no natural enemies and therefore the rifle is an important management tool. *Paul Wood, Irish Deer Society.*

Teachtadálus rex

My colleague, Deputy Joanna Tuffy, told me her four-year-old daughter is very interested in dinosaurs and fossils and that she would particularly like to see them. *Mary Upton, Labour's arts spokeswoman in the Dáil, on the continuing closure of the Natural History Museum.*

Bring her in here. *Olivia Mitchell TD.*

Flock off

I wouldn't hurt any animal. The rooks were driving me bananas. I respect animals and wildlife, but it was impossible to live in my house. It was getting to the stage where I'd have to move or do something. I couldn't live any more on my land. *Giancarlo Orlandi, Co. Louth, prosecuted for hanging a dead rook from a tree to discourage the attentions of its mates.*

LOST WORDS

You see, Minister, you inhabit your own monetary world where shortfalls are called pressures, where new money is called easement. It's a world of euphemisms. *Assembly member David McNarry, Ulster Unionist, berates Finance Minister Nigel Dodds.*

Of course in the case of Anglo Irish Bank the due diligence did lead to a change of mind. *Finance Minister Brian Lenihan.*

. . . after they got the €7 billion, that do jillence . . . do jillgence . . . would be undertaken. Is this government off its tree completely? That they do due jillens, do jill, diligence, only after they've given €7 billion. Isn't it mad? *Vincent Browne on the Ray D'Arcy Show.*

I'm not aware of any medical condition in which sexual activity is a recognised treatment

confesses Dr John Cuddihy during a public hearing in which a fellow GP *is accused of advising a female patient with a disturbed sleep pattern that the condition would be alleviated by recourse to a warm alcoholic drink, exercise, a good book or finding a 'willy' and having sex. There are, apparently, no such user-friendly antidotes on offer in respect of the continuing recession; BUT Ireland wins the rugby Grand Slam for the first time in all those years and both jurisdictions on this island still have hopes of the soccer World Cup. Cliché of the Month: 'transparency'. People are beginning to see through it.*

He'd had a vasectomy eight years before he came to shoot me—it's called transference, I think. Everything that went wrong in his life he blamed me for. His wife had left him; his life had begun to fall to pieces. *Dr Andrew Rynne, pioneer of vasectomy in Ireland, shot in the hip by an ungrateful patient.*

There is a French saying which, when translated, says, 'In getting old, you get more mad and more wise,' and people forget you get wiser. Older people tend to be sensible drivers. Their accident record is better than younger drivers every year. *Consultant geriatrician Professor Des O'Neill.*

HIS & HERS
Dublin is a great city to visit but it's hard to live in. I sometimes flippantly say, 'In Canada I get to forget I'm a lesbian for months on end.' It's great because you don't have to spend all your energy worrying about it; you get on with your life. Of course you can live in

Ireland and be gay, but I always get the feeling that you will be banging your head against the wall quite often. *Writer Emma Donoghue.*

Expressive male

In my days of playing it wasn't considered manly to hug or kiss other players when you scored a try. You just put your head down and trotted back to position to get on with it. Even though you may have felt elated internally, you certainly didn't show it. It's becoming far more prevalent in rugby now, which I suppose comes from soccer. But in rugby it's still the rugged hug, a 'bouncing off the chest' hug rather than anything more affectionate. *RTÉ's New Zealand rugby analyst Brent Pope.*

Aye fond Kiss . . .

I watched the boys jumping on the pitch for three to five seconds, then turned and we all suddenly enveloped into a group hug. A bit of man love. It doesn't hurt, does it? *Rugby defensive coach Les Kiss, overcome by the Grand Slam victory.*

Lift off

Everyone just seems to think I have spent thousands on cosmetic surgery. When I go out somewhere women will come up to me and actually ask straight to my face, 'Do you mind if I ask what is the work you have had done?' The truth is I haven't had a pick of surgery. *Entertainer Twink.*

Lady's choice

When I was about seven, I felt different. I felt like I wasn't like other boys. I felt more like a girl. I talked to girls easier. It was there right through my teens, but I couldn't put a name on it until much later. I knew I should have nothing down below. *Donegal farmer Sarah Louise Stafford, born a male.*

Ironing in the soul

The decision to become a stay-at-home dad is ideally one that should be actively and carefully considered. There is a growing awareness in society today that it is best for families if one parent can be at home to raise the children. While it is not traditionally a role occupied by men, there is no doubt that temperament rather than gender should be the deciding factor. *Brendan McKiernan, clinical psychotherapist, Bray, Co. Wicklow.*

No score
I was chatting to a guy in a bar, and when I said I played rugby, he just gave me a look and that was it. *Joy Neville, captain of the Ireland women's rugby squad.*

Bowler's pitch
The funny thing about this crisis is that it's a male crisis. There are very few women. I've only met two in this crisis—Gillian Bowler, the chair of Irish Life and Permanent, and the chairperson of the post-office bank. That's it. Everybody else, it's been men all the way. *Labour finance spokeswoman Joan Burton.*

Liberation theology
I agree absolutely with the Vatican. The first time I turned mine on, it was like having the best orgasm. I felt totally liberated. It was wonderful to get away from all that messing with twin tubs. *Liz McManus TD. The Vatican's Osservatore Romano claims that the washing machine has liberated women.*

The idea that we were all liberated by labour-saving devices is ludicrous. We already had the mindset there. The condom today is the best invention. *Author Claire Dowling.*

Boot camp
Since I got involved with the team, it has been, literally, make-up and clothes out the window. I am wearing jeans and wearing mucky wellies. I am freezing. There is not anything remotely glamorous doing 'Celebrity Bainisteoir'. But there is a sense of freedom about the whole thing. *Model Andrea Roche takes charge of a GAA team for the TV cameras.*

AN TEANGA BHEO
There wasn't the same level of industrialisation and modernisation here as there had been in other countries, so that when people began to get interested in folklore, we still had a lot of it. And that was true particularly in the Gaeltacht areas, where the language still survived

and there were people who could recite these huge long tales. *Anraí Ó Braonáin, president, Folklore of Ireland Society.*

The Irish language is definitely undergoing a revival among all age groups, and there's a huge interest in, and public support for, what we are doing. People are realising that being able to speak Irish is a huge asset. *Antoine Ó Coileáin, CEO, Gael Linn.*

We liked to apply our Irishness politically to promote the self-stereotype of being friendly, open, welcoming and having had an experience of being victims in past history. The reality is that we can also use our Irishness very strategically to keep people out. A language is about communication and about being able to communicate effectively—but a language that one can only speak to some people, and which excludes others, is by definition exclusive. *Professor Orla Muldoon, Department of Psychology, University of Limerick.*

ONLY A GAME
He was undoubtedly one of the most iconic sportsmen ever to come from Northern Ireland, so that's going to make the difference between what's a good price and an absolutely phenomenal price. *Richard Bell, Wilson's Auctioneers, Belfast, anticipating an auction of the effects of soccer star George Best.*

Roving commissioner
They do that every year—they don't like me coming here. All these people take their skiing holidays and winter holidays. This is what I do—Cheltenham. I never ever went on one of those Patrick's Day trips that ministers do—I said, 'I'm not goin' anywhere. I'm goin' to Cheltenham.' *EU commissioner Charlie McCreevy.*

From the jaws of defeat
I gave him a handkerchief I had in my shorts and he starts trying to dry the ball. Jesus you wouldn't have dried it with a vacuum cleaner. The crowd went berserk, booing, whistling, everything. And all Barney says is, 'Fuck 'em!' He calmly kicked the goal and I often think of that since, with all the coaching that goes on, Christ above in Heaven, we never had a coach. Rugby is a simple game. *Winning try scorer Paddy Reid on Barney Mullan's conversion at the Stade Colombes,*

Paris, 1948, on the way to Ireland's first Grand Slam, recalled on the eve of the second.

This will be the final act; it's come down to this. All the dreams and all the hopes and all the aspirations of this Irish Grand Slam effort on Stephen Jones making or not making this kick. *TV commentator Ryle Nugent.*

I was ready to kill Paddy. *Ronan O'Gara on Paddy Wallace's giving away the crucial penalty.*

I just felt the game lacked a bit of excitement. *Paddy Wallace.*

What a wonderful day and what a great pleasure to see Ireland have this deserved win. They have toiled hard. They have had their Triple Crowns in the past and now they will have the pleasure of being members of a Grand Slam Team for the rest of their lives. *Out-half Jackie Kyle, key member of the 1948 team.*

If Kidney had gone for religion instead of teaching he would have been Pope. *Commentator George Hook on the Irish team trainer.*

Hoops realised

For as long as I've been following Rovers, people have asked why I support them when they were a mess, no success. But you follow them for this. The older lads had the glory days. This is the start of the glory days for us. *Rowan McFeedy, returning from the US to see Shamrock Rovers soccer club christen their new Tallaght Stadium after 22 years of peripatetic existence.*

It's just been such a long journey, and plenty of people who started out with us didn't make it. I don't want to think too much about what it means, because it's just so big to us. *Lifelong Hoops fan and club PRO John Byrne.*

Hurling insults

The threat against my life, which has been referred to the Gardaí, is the latest in a sequence of threats and abuse, random or organised I do not know, which I and my family members have had to endure. *Cork hurling coach Gerald McCarthy resigns.*

That man has been through hell and back. He only ever had the interest of Cork GAA at heart and I think he had had to put up with an unbelievable amount of stress. And for a man who has given so much to Cork, I think it was terrible what he had to go through. *GAA president Nickey Brennan.*

But most of the fans of the current team would only know these guys as leading hurlers. Some of them wouldn't know our hurlers of the past. To some of these fans, Christy Ring is a roundabout on the outer city road. This is the current generation and they have taken a good man apart . . . *Former Cork hurler Tony Connolly.*

MAMMON

I am totally opposed to the hysterical campaign that has been whipped up against the banking system as a whole. There are delinquents within the banking system and people who should be bought to book and, indeed, put in jail. The Bank of Ireland, however, has existed since before the Famine . . . Allied Irish Bank goes back to the Munster and Leinster Bank, and no one would wish to see these two great Irish institutions, which have a physical presence in every town and village, go to the wall. *Senator Eoghan Harris.*

His conduct shows little care for savers who have placed considerable faith—and in some cases, placed their life's chances and the fortunes of their families—in the care of that institution. *Dan Boyle, Green Party, on Irish Nationwide chief executive Michael Fingleton.*

I have come here to look at the golden circle—the people with the brass necks who have yet to be held to account. They should have all been cleared out. They seem to be running a private Ireland for themselves. *Mick Lawlor, Ballsbridge, Dublin, at the Bank of Ireland AGM.*

My message to the white-collar criminals—with their champagne-and-caviar lifestyle—is very simple: you won't get away with it. You will be pursued. You will be held to account. You will face the full rigours of the law. And you will pay for what you have done to our country. *Green Party leader John Gormley.*

Lord Protectus

There's no parallel in history for the damage they have done to this nation—except perhaps Cromwell. And even Cromwell was motivated by reasons other than personal gain. *Minister Noel Dempsey at the Fianna Fáil Ard Fheis.*

Borderline cases

I have no problem with Southern retailers getting a good kicking. Look at the border regions between France and Germany and Holland and Germany, where people adjust their spending habits literally every week. What we need is an 'equalised' market in Europe, but we don't have one on this island yet. *Former IBEC chairman Maurice Healy.*

LESSER BREEDS

Would you believe it? There it is, laid out in front of us. The body of the Celtic Tiger. Shot by the British. *Sinn Féin Deputy Arthur Morgan, emerging from the Dáil, is confronted by a stuffed feline being removed from the adjacent Natural History Museum.*

Creature comfort

If there is a traumatised animal that nobody can touch then they call me. I go and apply everything I know. I will tilt my head and move like the animal. I will make high pitch noises and become more animal-like than human. In this way I can show them that I am not an enemy. If I know an animal is dangerous I will walk in backwards to the cage to show that I am not a threat. It is very logical and probably a German approach. *Thomas Kanak, Ballymore Eustace, Co. Wicklow, dog whisperer.*

Doing bird

I specifically want to reach kids with special needs, who are on the way—troubled, deprived children, the kids who'd be veering off into crime fairly fast. That's another area to go and capture. I guarantee you, if you can put falconry into their lives, it can wean them away from crime. *Trevor 'The Hawk Man' Roche, Dublin Falconry.*

PARTY LINES
We can't go on forever-and-a-day excusing people in the public sector earning huge salaries making mistakes and simply walking away from them. To suggest that people always find ways to defraud the public is not the correct attitude. It smacks of complacency. *East Derry Assembly member John Dallat.*

Firm footing
There's such a thing as political rhetoric. I admire anyone from a political party who can stand up on a stone wall and say what they stand for . . . *Labour TD Michael D. Higgins.*

Up the Republic
I want to once again state that Éirigí is an open, independent, democratic political party which is not aligned to, or supportive of, any armed organisation. We in Éirigí do not believe that the conditions exist at this time for a successful armed struggle against the British occupation. *Party spokesman Brian Leeson.*

Up the Republicans
Most of the 'serious operators' around Cullyhanna left long ago. The central ones, the best of them, are now doing nothing, totally left it behind and have no interest in it. But there are now young men—and girls too—who don't give a tuppenny fuck about the IRA or Sinn Féin and will tell them that. They are even beginning to take the piss out of the hard men. *Former Armagh Sinn Féin councillor Jim McAllister.*

Wee want
I have come to the conclusion that the UUP does not have the interests of Conservatism at heart. Rather, as the UUP is facing a severe financial crisis, it sees the Conservatives as a means out of its financial and electoral woes. Many UUP members (although by no means all) still adopt a little Ulster mentality when it comes to politics, and the party's only MP is simply not a Conservative. *NI Conservative Jeffrey Peale.*

HERE & THERE
In terms of our national or international credibility, if anything is pulled on the Metro at this moment, we can throw our hat at trying

to attract those kinds of players to invest here in the future. *Tom Parlon, Construction Industry Federation.*

Drain brain

Afterwards I went back into the pub and laughed it off. In all seriousness, though, I have to say a huge thank you to the emergency services here and the Melbourne fire brigade. They were brilliant about it all. It was a much bigger job than you would think. *Julie Halton, released from a draining two-hour experience.*

To have an Irish woman with her arm trapped down a drain outside an Irish pub, well, it's probably got to be St Patrick's Day. *Melbourne fire fighter Darren McQuade.*

Netting the surfer

Being Irish myself I was intrigued when I heard about this character. But when people heard about it they thought I was completely bonkers. They said, 'An Irish guy started the surf scene? You've got to be crazy!' But it's true. *Joel Conroy, director of surfing documentary 'Waveriders', discovers that the sport owes its Hawaiian origin partly to Ulster's George Freeth.*

THAR LEAR

We wanted to do something very affectionate that was about us hearing about Ireland for years and we come over here and it isn't quite the way we imagined but it's still really nice. I first visited in 2001 and what I couldn't believe was how technologically forward Ireland was— it was so amazing to me. *'The Simpsons' producer Al Jean on the making of an Irish episode.*

Ould Orange Fruit

Jaysis, Ian, it wouldn't do for you of all people to be choked to death by an orange. *RTÉ's Charlie Bird to Ian Paisley Junior, whose citric breakfast sticks in his gullet in New York's Fitzpatrick's Hotel.*

O'Bama arís

He doesn't want to dilute his brand by introducing other nationalities. He has told a very powerful story about growing up bi-racial. If he adds the Irish piece, that message gets distorted . . . He was secretly

born in Co. Cork to a Muslim leprechaun. We read it in Wikipedia!
Darrell West, vice-president, Brookings Institute.

We have a few connections in the international suit trade. The
President has had suits made to order; we got his size through the
grapevine. Can't say any more than that. *Adrian Copeland, whose firm,
Louis Copeland, made a Donegal tweed jacket for the President for St
Patrick's Day.*

When I was a relatively unknown candidate for office, I didn't know
about this part of my heritage, which would have been very helpful in
Chicago. So I thought I was bluffing when I put the apostrophe after
the O. I tried to explain that 'Barack' was an ancient Celtic name. *An
t-Uachtarán.*

Kick in the Derrière
Foley's NY Pub wants Danny Boy to sing a happier song in 2009. Times
are tougher for a lot of people, so we're looking for a little levity.
Instead of banning Danny Boy, we're trying to put a happier ending
on what is one of the world's saddest songs. *Co. Cavan pub owner
Shaun Clancy, who banned the Londonderry Air in 2008, announces a
$500 competition.*

RECESSIONAL
None of them want to go back to Poland because, first of all, there's
no jobs, and secondly, they have families there and they don't want to
go home and say, 'I've failed.' They say, 'How can I say to my wife and
children that I lost my job?' *Joanna Rekas, Dublin Simon homeless
shelter.*

Ere Aer
An analyst told us that he was talking to an economist in the Fed
[Federal Reserve] who said it is going to be the worst worldwide
recession since 1872. I said that is pretty bad for us because there was
no aviation in 1872. *Alan Joyce, Irish boss of Qantas.*

Roll on, roll off
We are having to adapt our breakfast offering to the new world. The
sale of breakfast rolls is down probably in line with the decline in the

construction industry. I won't say breakfast roll man is dead but he's not as high-viz as he was. *Topaz chairman Neil O'Leary.*

Women and children first

This market doesn't get too affected by the recession because it's genuine collectors and, to be honest, they'd probably hock the wife and children to buy what they want. *Auctioneer Ian Whyte, selling Michael Collins memorabilia.*

MURDER MOST FOUL

We don't want to go back to this. Nobody wants to go back to this in any way at all. None of us wants it in any way at all and we pray that those who are engaged in this will just stop it. Go away from it. We don't want those years of the past. They were horrible years for everyone. *Fr Tony Devlin, Antrim, on the killings by dissident Republicans at Massereene barracks.*

Because of the way in this society we often refer to events by place names, when people talk about Antrim in the future they will think of Saturday night. But that wasn't Antrim. Antrim was Sunday lunchtime, the people standing in simple, quiet dignity as an expression of sympathy to the soldiers who had lost their lives. *Alliance Party leader David Ford.*

He thought this war was over, but obviously not, and I just can't believe this has all started up again. If Steve's death has made a positive effect on all of this, that's all I care about. *Kate Carroll on her husband, PSNI Constable Stephen Carroll, murdered by the Continuity IRA.*

It is regrettable that anyone has to lose their life, but the reality is that when we have occupation within a country there is a very deep resistance, including armed resistance. We have always upheld the right of the Irish people to use any level of controlled legitimate force to drive the British out of Ireland. *Richard Walsh, publicity director, Republican Sinn Féin.*

These people are traitors to the island of Ireland. They have betrayed the political desire, hopes and aspirations of all the people who live on this island and they don't deserve to be supported by anyone. *Deputy First Minister Martin McGuinness.*

CHURCH & STATE
There is not one person on this planet who understands what transubstantiation actually means. So to use it as the actual flagship, to say if you don't subscribe to this then you're out, is to me anti-Christian. *Mark Patrick Hederman, Abbot of Glenstal Abbey.*

Mighty Mouse
When you think about it, we're a Mickey Mouse island with a population of about six million. But just look at the coverage we got this week, right around the world. When you see Ireland on the globe, we're just a tiny pinprick and yet you see our tentacles all over the place. *Frank McGee, Dublin Tourism, celebrates St Patrick's Day.*

Germination once again
In the past, the Catholic church sent missionaries all over the world, particularly to Africa. The Bible teaches us the same principle—where the seed goes, the harvest will come. So, in the Republic of Ireland a lot of us have come back as the harvest for the seed that was planted. *Pastor Tunde Adebayo-Oke, Pentecostal Church in Ireland.*

Nod and a wink
Ireland has long suffered from high levels of undue or hidden influence over regulation and government, by vested interests. We've seen over the last few years a relatively large number of cases of what could be referred to as legal corruption, or efforts to subvert or undermine due process in policy making. *John Devitt, Transparency International.*

Cross purposes
When I was 14, I got a job in a factory … He put me sitting at this desk and on this desk there was little crosses and figures and little types of ribbons and a small little tiny hammer. And he showed me what to do, actually nailing Christ on the cross. I done that all day, hammering Christ on the cross, and when I went home that evening my mother said to me, 'Well how did you get on? What were you doing?' I said, 'I didn't like it so much. I was hammering Christ on the cross.' *Dubliner Mary Moffatt.*

It will be done in a fun, lighthearted way. A lot of young people forget what Easter is really about. This is a way of reminding them. *Peter May, owner of a Wexford nightclub, planning a mock crucifixion on the dance floor.*

Averse to The Boss

He was a very capable civil servant—'my private secretary the poet'. I must say I basked in it. I wasn't directly written about; he focused on more notable people than me. He had some remarkable things to say about Charles J. Haughey. *T.K. Whitaker on Tom Kinsella's sojourn in the Department of Finance.*

The bare thing

When the paper asked him if he would continue to bathe nude while mayor of Limerick, Clem replied, 'No, I'll be wearing my chain of office.' *Gerry Casey on his late father.*

SOCIAL & PERSONAL

I see the girls falling for these mini-gangsters and some of these young men are treated like heroes. It's the only status they can get in life. It's the stuff of fiction but it's actually reality. *Parish priest Fr Séamus Ahern, on Finglas, Dublin, gang murderers.*

Strings attached

We were two of the largest students the world had ever seen living together in one of the smallest bedsits the world had ever seen. There was no fridge, and we cooled our wine tied to a string in the lavatory cistern. *4FM and former RTÉ presenter Derek Davis recalls student days at Queen's with colleague Tom McGurk.*

Pubic interest

People are very happy to look at Britney's genitals on the internet but they don't want anyone seeing their wheelie bins. *Frank Skinner on Google's proposed Street View of Dublin.*

House and home

In Donegal, if they offer you a house and you look for Traveller-specific accommodation, they deem you to be awkward. You wait a long time, then you have children so you take the house they are offering. But you are not allowed have your dogs, your horses or your traditions; that's how the culture disappears. *Hughie Friel, Donegal Travellers Project.*

Spirit leveller
Our goal at the end of the day is to help people who think their house or structure is haunted. Unlike some groups we won't go into a house and just say, 'Yes, your house is haunted and good luck with that.' We strive to find a logical explanation and that is usually enough to satisfy our clients. As our founder Ian Murphy once said, 'Nine times out of ten our clients need a plumber, not a priest.' *David Winger, Paranormal Research Association of Ireland.*

ARTS & PARTS
To have met and gotten to work with an actress as bright and brilliant as Anna on my very first play was one of the most rewarding experiences of my whole life. She was one of the true greats of Irish stage and screen and a lovely woman, and I'll miss her. *Playwright Michael McDonagh on Anna Manahan, who died this month.*

Liam Shakespeare
The evidence that it represents Shakespeare and that it was done from life, though it is circumstantial, is in my view overwhelming. *Professor Stanley Wells, general editor,* The Oxford Shakespeare, *on a portrait discovered in Newbridge House, Fingal.*

Evening devotion
Ten years of hosting this marvellous institution of Irish broadcasting. It's been an absolute joy; however, all good things come to an end. And I have decided, after consultation with my family, that it's about time I spent Friday nights at home. *'Late Late' presenter Pat Kenny.*

I'm just glad I will have him around on Friday nights while I am still young enough to enjoy him. *Mrs Kathy Kenny.*

Buffo
They're not very sophisticated images, but they do represent someone's disgust at, not necessarily Brian Cowen, but Brian Cowen as a figurehead of the Government. And the thing about satire is, it's not supposed to be funny. Ultimately, it's a catharsis . . . *Cartoonist Allan*

Cavanagh on nude portraits of the Taoiseach by Conor Casby found hanging in two Dublin art galleries.

At a time when the majority of gangland murders remain unsolved, to have Gardaí spending their time investigating what amounted to a practical joke that offended the Taoiseach's ego is a scandalous waste of resources. *Fine Gael justice spokesman Charlie Flanagan.*

Deputy Kenny will have to resume his seat because I am not going into that nonsense at all. The deputy should stop it. That is for the *Dandy* and such like. *The Ceann Comhairle on the Fine Gael leader's attempt to raise the matter in the Dáil.*

Not taking it lying down
Bob always said he wanted to be in the Boomtown Rats to get rich, famous and laid. I just loved music. That's ultimately why we parted company. Our music became secondary. *Band co-founder Gerry Cott.*

Swings (low) and arrows
What happens when an industry starts disappearing—and I'm sure it was the same for chariot makers or longbow makers—is that all the back-up systems around you start disappearing. I've been saying this for about five years now, but there's a real problem that we don't make anything any more in this country. Not the clothes, not the carpets, not the nails in the floor. *Former fashion designer and gallery owner Michael Mortell.*

D4mation
When I started in AA Roadwatch I would get teased for being a culchie. But to be honest, I think that 'rindabite' thing was actually created by people who came in there before me. But at the same time, the AA Roadwatch girls were the first 'radio babes'. So I think it worked out well for me to be the first with a western accent. *98FM presenter and Sligo girl Louise Heraghty.*

EUROPA AND THE BULL
We need now to develop in Europe much greater public consciousness of the overall cultural—and eventual political—implications of the emergence of a distinctive European value system

which I believe corresponds very closely to the instinctive value system of Irish people. *Former Taoiseach Garret FitzGerald.*

Pint taken

Being a pop singer, I have to learn incrementalism very slowly, but I'm trying to get him pissed so we can move things along more quickly. *Anti-poverty activist Bob Geldof meets EU Commission president José Mañuel Barroso over a Patrick's Day Guinness or two.*

Paying through the 'no's

It is very difficult to see any country being able to stay in if they have had two Nos from the people. It would be very difficult to get large companies to invest in a country that looked as if it might be leaving the EU. *British Liberal MEP Graham Watson.*

A second 'No' would have horrific consequences for Ireland and I am not the first to say it. *German Ambassador Christian Pauls.*

TAILPIECE

I'm a year younger than Mickey Mouse. *Octogenarian poet John Montague.*

April 2009

I do get some quirky requests

says Susan Bevan, founder of Dublin Barter Club: 'I had a woman contact me recently who wanted someone to teach her Spanish, Pilates and wolf-whistling. So I said that I'd do my best to find her someone who would teach her one, or the other, or all. Anyway, I asked a member and he said that he didn't need any barter from her but in the spirit of the bartering club, he would teach her to wolf-whistle.' As Liam Shakespeare puts it, 'Age cannot wither her, nor custom stale/Her infinite variety.' There follow equally informative insights into the world of mná na hÉireann. *Cliché of the Month: 'vibrant'; surely the fabric of society is shaky enough.*

We badly need the women of 1916 back again to shake up the political system. There is a very, very strong case for a memorial in recognition of the contribution of women to the 1916 Rising and beyond. *Noirín Byrne, granddaughter of a captain in the Citizen Army.*

Same difference
If you talk to adolescent girls, they'll deny the clone look. Put them in a room and they look like mirror images of each other but in their minds they are saying, 'We're all individual. We're all unique.' What they are doing is creating a 'them and us' scenario: this is us and God forbid that a mother or a teacher would wear something trendy. *Educational psychologist Nicky O'Leary.*

Brain drain
I came up with the idea because people were constantly picking my brains for legal advice. They didn't want the rigmarole of going to a solicitor's office and forking out the huge rates. During the boom years, people became scared of lawyers and the mad money they were charging. That is the sort of stereotype I'm trying to break down. I'm just a regular girl. I don't think I'm anything special just because I

happen to be a solicitor. *Rachel McDaid, founder of Legal Line, information phone service.*

Unhappy medium
It was a real baptism of fire. It was really tough. I thought I was already out there, but when I went on radio I was absolutely shocked by the attention—getting the papers and finding you are being reviewed, and not very favourably, and finding that maybe sometimes they are right. *RTÉ 'Drivetime' presenter and former TV reporter Mary Wilson.*

Homo sapiens
Irish women are still wearing L-plates in fashion. In Ireland the fact that real style is about doing simple things often gets lost under a pile of undernourished hair, unnecessary jewellery, unfortunate layering, unsuitable underwear, unschooled use of makeup and unscrupulous use of fake tan. *Eddie Shanahan, former Arnotts, Dublin, marketing director.*

Homo erectus
I stand up when a woman enters a room. It does provoke a negative reaction in some quarters but I do it regardless of the reaction. *Writer Robert O'Byrne.*

BRICKS & MORTAR
They are the new poor. They can't eat their bricks and mortar. A big part of the problem is that property values are so over-rated by estate agents and the banks, who can't afford to reflect the worthlessness in the balance sheet. *Wicklow councillor Irene Winters on the plight of the asset-rich self-employed, disqualified from benefits.*

Inclined to differ
They knock on walls, stick screwdrivers through wallpapered walls and even remove skirting boards looking for damp. It's a nightmare, and parents of first-time buyers are the worst. They come along to give their children advice but . . . one parent told me that the house was sinking and started rolling coins along the floor trying to prove that the property had subsided. *John Newcombe, Newcombe Estates, Castleknock, Co. Dublin.*

Happy returns

For a long time, people were getting letters in the door saying, 'The interest rate on your mortgage is going up.' Now the letters are saying, 'Your interest rates are going down.' That is certainly taking effect. We have noticed that some people working in Dublin who moved well outside the capital, because it was what they could afford at the time, are now seeing that they can afford to move closer to their work and cut their commuting time. *Estate agent Ian McCarthy, Sherry Fitzgerald.*

When I left this house 30 years ago I was absolutely convinced I would never be coming back; usually in the passage of one's career it's rare to get back to the same railway station, let alone the same train. Despite all that's happened in the interval it's been a huge advantage that I've walked up and down so many more avenues, more staircases and through so many more doors. *Conservation architect John O'Connell returns to Fota House, Co. Cork (which adjoins a railway station).*

Starting blocks

It takes people's minds off the mortgage, bills and work and, while it can be childish, it is also very creative and very technical. Many architects and builders started off with Lego. *Gerald Bedell, tutor at Belfast's Lego Factor evening classes—for adults.*

Drawering the line

You can spend three or four months designing a building so that the details are really crisp, only to have the aesthetic destroyed by five pairs of knickers hanging on a line. *Architect Dermot Bannon on apartment developments.*

CÉAD MÍLE FÁILTE

Our passengers are from all around the world, but you can make some generalisations. I love Americans, because they ask me things like 'What's that guy doing over there, Declan?' Obviously, I don't have a clue, so I tell them he's a Nobel prize winner for being out standing in his field. *Declan Somers, Galway Tour Company.*

Fare play

I said, 'Look, I am doing the same job as you guys and you are part of a union.' I said, 'What are the conditions?' and he said, 'No, the union is just for the Irish.' *Guinean Lama Niankowe is refused membership of the Cork Taxi Drivers' Association.*

Hi Brazil
They dovetailed well with life here because they moved from one rural place to another. And they were welcomed because they were seen as saviours of the local meat industry. More than half of them have gone, but some have remained. There will be a Brazilian aspect of life in Gort from now on. *Frank Murray, Gort, Co. Galway, Family Resource Centre.*

Pole position
We are the second-largest immigrant community, so it's very important that our voice will be heard—that Polish people will say what are their issues, what are their hopes, what are the challenges in the local communities where they live. You don't want a particular community to be marginalised just because nobody can hear what we have to say. *Emilia Marchelewska, Forum Polonia.*

Soon it will be quite obvious that Poles in Ireland are not the same as Poles in Poland. *Professor John Berry, Ontario, Canada.*

Dead end
The Chair of the meeting and I were surrounded by an angry mob, who shouted, among other things, that I was a 'murderer', a 'Nazi', and had no respect for human life. One person next to me said that if I tried to speak, he would personally stop me and that I was not welcome there or anywhere else in Ireland. *Visiting Professor Len Doyal attempts to lecture on euthanasia at Cork University Hospital.*

Wicklow way
Living here for the past 15 years, there has been complete harmony in my life. I have been completely absorbed into the nobility of the Wicklow hills around me. This is the place where I have planted myself. It is a refuge where I restore myself. *Actor Daniel Day-Lewis accepts the first Freedom of Wicklow award.*

FAITH & MORALS
The search for God is one of the reasons to be alive! To declare oneself an atheist is paradoxically an act of faith because it presupposes some

kind of knowledge that there isn't a God. The truth about it is I would be more agnostic than atheist because I can't actually prove anything. *Actor Gabriel Byrne.*

Benefit of clergy
We gave out free jackets to priests. They'd get a free jacket if they bought so much. We thought it was a good idea. But there was war when we gave out the jackets. If one priest got one, and another saw it then he wanted a jacket. They're like children. *Dessie Wisley, Wisley Ecclesiastical Supplies.*

Repeat performance
Well, you know the song, 'Everybody Knew, but Nobody Said', about Anne Lovett. That's the thing, we all know but we don't say. Everybody knows what was wrong with the country over the last ten years, but we still vote them back in. If Bertie came back next week, he'd be fuckin' re-elected. So would Charlie. Jesus! *Singer Christy Moore.*

MAMMON
Fianna Fáil has taken a massive €90 billion gamble on behalf of the taxpayer in bailing out the very property speculators and banks that dragged our economy over a cliff in the last few years. *Fine Gael finance spokesman Richard Bruton is worried by the establishment of Nama, the National Asset Management Agency.*

Past tents
I don't envisage that Nama will have a tent at any famous Irish race-course. *Finance Minister Brian Lenihan suggests that the new agency will not be at the races.*

Home truths
We are warning people to be particularly cautious when responding to work-from-home job adverts. Our advice is that if a job seems too good to be true, it usually is. *Ann Fitzgerald, National Consumer Agency.*

Opportunity knockered
Some of those people who write those articles, you know, if they had have employed as many people in this country; if they had have put

themselves at risk, and their personal wealth into banks. It's easier, as you and I know, Derek, to be the knocker who never did anything, never created a job, and then just be there using the cynical factor. *Former Taoiseach Bertie Ahern speaks to interviewer Derek Davis.*

Every which witch
I was in the Conrad hotel earlier this year and Michael Fingleton came in alone. I was proud to stand up and shake his hand. He gave me my first mortgage. When he mightn't have. When I wasn't the most solvent person in Ireland. And I think if you're going to do witch-hunts, you should do your own personal ones. Pick your own people. *Writer Colm Tóibín.*

SHADES OF GREEN
I didn't think much in the beginning about being British or Irish. Okay, I lived in the North. I had a British scholarship. I carried a British passport to go to Lourdes, so the double identity was something that you lived with. *Septuagenarian Seamus Heaney recollects.*

I have an Irish passport. I've an out-of-date British passport. I always race with the Irish licence because it's cheaper. But I think Ulster is a very different part of Ireland. I used to believe in the united Ireland but now I don't because we are very different. *Former Formula 1 driver Eddie Irvine.*

London pride
While some who represent nationalists continue their paranoid and manic drive to obliterate the term 'Londonderry' from everyday usage, the Government which they ascribe loyalty to has abandoned attempting to force the inaccurate and offensive term on those who do not wish to use it. *DUP MLA Gregory Campbell on the Republic's decision to accept both 'Derry' and 'Londonderry' on passports issued to Stroke City's natives.*

I couldn't care less that my children don't know their Irish roots. And I would probably not live in Ireland again because I feel at home in London. *Bob Geldof.*

Shades of screen

Television is a copycat business. It would be incredibly arrogant of me to say that we didn't make some shows that we shouldn't have made. Of course we did. But I think now, even more than before, as resources get tighter and digital penetration grows we need to constantly ask, 'Is this programme really distinctively Irish?' *Noel Curran, RTÉ television head.*

'ATIN' & DRINKIN'

There's too much snobbery about restaurants. I hate going into posh restaurants. I hate going into a restaurant that is full of suits. I hate it. I hate the concept that the only people who can afford a restaurant is a bunch of boring old businessmen, who spend all their time talking about some stupid Bordeaux wine only they can afford. *Mayo-born London restaurateur Oliver Peyton.*

Foreign currency

I felt in essence that what was happening with the disappearance of the traditional pub was that certain values that are important to the Irish and Irish identity were kind of losing their currency, and being replaced by some of the less attractive aspects of American culture. That rapid influx of money, people getting rich very quickly. *US writer Bill Barich.*

Deportment of the Taoiseach

I gave Jack a terrible time about him being the reason why we were always broke, and for our first official party we invited him and Maureen across the road. He arrived with two bottles of Château Lynch-Bages, saying that they were 'from the family vineyard'! He knew that we couldn't afford anything that expensive and it has always had a special place in my heart since. I still toast Jack and miss him. *Pianist John O'Connor on near neighbour and then Taoiseach Jack Lynch.*

Ill-starred

I can't speak for other Michelin-starred restaurants in Ireland but for me at the moment, it's all about survival. The Michelin star is the last thing in my head. In fact, having a Michelin star in a recession is about the worst thing you can have. *Chef Dylan McGrath, closing his Dublin restaurant.*

Fizzible improvement
This is more about refreshment and zing. The stout has a different look and taste than anything our fans have ever experienced, but still retains the familiar character. *Guinness master brewer Fergal Murray on a new carbonated product aimed at the US market.*

Penalty claws
We are very proud of Bram but he died 25 years before I was born so I never met him . . . the family background to the writing of *Dracula* was a dinner of dressed crab and a terrible nightmare. *Bram Stoker's great-grandson Noel Dobbs.*

Egging them on
Feeding is the thing, the best of everything—carrots, peas, tomatoes, yoghurts, meat, nuts, salmon, only the best. Salmon for breakfast, a bit of cereal, yoghurt, the occasional boiled egg, never raw—I'd be big into body temperature, into bloods, and if you give them a raw egg it's like putting it into a hot radiator in a car (an old emergency trick for a leaking rad); it seals everything. *Greyhound trainer Pat Buckley.*

ARTS & PARTS
We haven't really gone back to the well, and a lot of people compare the end of the Celtic Tiger to waking up with a massive hangover. I think home-grown is where it's at. Do what you do really well. Be distinctive and unique. What's the point in aping something that you can get on 20 other channels? *Former RTÉ 'Late Late' researcher Donal Scannell.*

Arts & farts
I'm always interested in telling the story with good acting. The play is the thing. All my life I've been accused of being populist, but I don't think you can do theatre unless people go to it. I've no time for the arty-farty wanky stuff that goes on, such as conceptualising. It's about telling stories and telling them well. *Actor and producer Joe Dowling.*

Late Late latest
I don't want the 'Late Late Show' job. Why would I want it? I don't even live in the same fucking country. *Broadcaster Dara Ó Briain.*

I couldn't be the next host of the 'Late Late Show' because RTÉ wouldn't offer it to me. RTÉ hasn't even asked me if I would be interested in being the presenter of the 'Late Late Show'. *Broadcaster Gerry Ryan.*

This is painful for me because I love talking and I am by nature an indiscreet person. I kind of think life is about talking, but on this I'm being a saint. *Broadcaster Miriam O'Callaghan refrains from commenting on her 'Late Late' prospects.*

Non-committal
I was 16 when I got a script for *The Commitments* and I was to go for an audition. I remember I was sitting at the kitchen table, doing my homework, and my mam looked at me and said, 'No. You're going to stay in school and finish your Leaving Cert. Nothing will come of a movie with language like that in it.' *Singer Imelda May.*

Booking the cooks
I would argue that one strange result of the English taking our language from us was to set up a fiercely competitive revenge campaign, directed towards achieving more eloquence than standard English will ever achieve. English sounds, as they say, like people fighting in the kitchen. *Playwright Tom MacIntyre.*

Admission of gilt
You can find old paintings and prints at auctions like Buckleys, and often the frames are quite good. It's cheap to buy *National Geographic* and cut out a photograph using a Stanley knife. It can look quite outrageous in a big gilt frame. *Interior designer Gregory Cullen.*

SPORTING CHANCES
Some of our players had arrived in Ireland when they were very young. They had never played a game of cricket, but cricket was in their blood. I got a feeling what it must have been like in Gaelic Park in New York for the Irish who arrived there. *John Corcoran, Ballaghaderreen Cricket Club, on the Pakistani contribution.*

Lunster final
My mother is from Cork and my father, who's from Kildare, went to school in Rockwell College in Tipperary so I was born into Munster

rugby. I have absolutely no affinity for Leinster and the D4 perception is very much there. I never felt part of that whole world, so I can't identify with it. *Kildare IT worker Joe King, living in Dublin.*

I just don't understand how somebody could turn their back on where they're from. If you're from Leinster, you should support Leinster. Simple as that. It is not a club for Dublin—or south Dublin—or whatever way you'd like to put it, but for the entire province. *Former Leinster and Ireland winger Denis Hickie.*

Pitch and boss

I intend to help an association badly handicapped by a lack of grass pitches. Nearly all the local league matches are played on all-weather pitches. It rains 260 days of the year and the temperature is rarely over 10 degrees but it is an extraordinary place with natural, unspoiled qualities. *Former Republic of Ireland boss Brian Kerr puts a brave face on his new role as manager of the Faroe Islands soccer team.*

There are moments a coach needs to take a stone and throw it at the water so that—Boom! Everything changes. *Current Ireland soccer boss Giovanni Trapattoni.*

There is no question. Roy is more than capable of being the Irish manager somewhere down the line—if that's something he wants to do . . . But Roy has a bigger job ahead of that at the moment at Ipswich, which is going out there and proving himself again. *Former Republic of Ireland player Ray Houghton.*

If I wasn't up for a challenge here I'd be out walking my dogs. My dogs need a break. *Roy Keane.*

A LITTLE LEARNING

Like Michael O'Leary's airports, Ireland's class sizes are miles away from where they should be. *John Carr, General Secretary, Irish National Teachers' Organisation.*

Tongue-tied

It felt real weird because they could all speak different languages and we could not. They were probably looking at us like we were disadvantaged. Even the ones from England could speak five languages. *Sarah Mahon, Dunboyne, Co. Meath, on a school visit to the European Parliament at Strasbourg.*

Hissing fit

An old man in Donegal once told me that the art of taxation lies in so plucking the goose as to get the largest amount of feathers with the least amount of hissing. Delegates, I don't have to tell you we are being well and truly plucked, and if we don't start hissing soon, the few feathers we have left will soon be gone. *Manus Brennan, Teachers Union of Ireland, at its annual conference.*

SOCIAL & PERSONAL

I just live from day to day. I don't drink, except maybe a wee Bailey's. I've never smoked and I only ever had one man. I feel good that I have been allowed to stay so long and I thank God my mind's clear. *Maria McQuillan, Belfast, cerebrating her 107th birthday.*

Good bad and indifferent

Injustice to me is injustice. Right is right. Wrong is wrong. I'm kind of simple to understand. I suppose a lot of people would say, 'Yeah, that's grand, any eejit can take the simple route.' Well, that's the approach I take; grey areas to me are an opting-out situation. What's going on in Darfur today is wrong. *John O'Shea of Goal.*

Orders and declarations

We want it to be broader and to recognise outstanding achievements across a wide area. It's a matter of meeting with relevant Government departments and the President's office and figuring out what the best way forward is. *Mary Davis, Office of Active Citizenship, involved in planning a national honours programme.*

I'm delighted as I've never got anything like this before. I got a gold medal from the Brazilian Academy of Letters, but I think that was a case of mistaken identity. *Senator David Norris, accepting a Lord Mayor's Award for a 'Special Contribution to Dublin'.*

Island bling

In a way, Ireland is quite provincial and there's that nouveau riche thing of showing your money and wearing the obvious labels—that's what 'going out' style in Ireland is all about. In other countries, maybe where they're used to having money, they tend to dress down. *Sunday Tribune fashion editor Ciara Elliott.*

PARTY LINES
I have confidence that Brian has the ability. He's a decent family man who understands the normal troubles of people's lives but he needs to shift his mindset from being the leader of Fianna Fáil to having a clear understanding that he is now the leader of the country. *Demoted junior minister John McGuinness.*

It's just sour grapes and he should take it on the chin like a man. *Niall Blaney TD.*

Under a cloud
The Government should respect the one million smokers in the country and not denigrate them at every turn. They are good cash cows for revenue and should be treated with respect and not as the Government usually treats them in this House. *Confirmed smoker Emmet Stagg TD.*

ROAD RUNNERS
There has been less pressure on the major routes into our cities, especially Dublin, in the last few months. The first quarter of the year was conspicuously quieter than previous years. It's something of a silver lining to the economic downturn. We may yet come to remember the gridlock of the Tiger era with something akin to nostalgia. *AA policy director Conor Faughnan.*

Non-runners
It's extremely short-sighted of the Government to cut funding for Dublin Bus precisely when demand will increase because of the recession and increased traffic congestion in the city centre due to infrastructural projects such as the proposed Metro and Luas extension. *Michael Faherty, General Secretary, National Bus & Rail Union.*

Simply placing a set of blue beacons and Garda signs on a vehicle does not make it a patrol car any more than placing a donkey in a stable would make it a racehorse. *Sergeant Séamus Burke, Louth Garda Division.*

Wheeling and dealing

I met the owner of the land in the pub and he liked the car I was driving, an Aston Martin DB24, and we made the swap over a couple of whiskeys. *Former racing driver John Gould, who exchanged his car for a plot of land on the Ring of Kerry, now seeking to swap it for a Bentley Continental GT.*

Suiting themselves

There are drivers out there who would drive up to the second floor of Brown Thomas and park their cars in the menswear section . . . I hope I got the right floor. *Green Party TD Ciarán Cuffe (Menswear is in the basement).*

Rainbow coalition

We have two different sets of traffic wardens. The usual fellas in the brown, and then there's the ones in the black with the red stripe. They don't give people a minute. You get situations where someone is dropping an old lady off to the hairdresser's and they are on top of them as soon as they stop. *Dún Laoghaire fishmonger Patricia Smith.*

Motorvation

Why do we put up with it? Why do we sit in our half-tonnes of metal, individualised, separated every day? Why do we allow it to continue, year in, year out, and spend monies to encourage that? *Green Party Minister Eamon Ryan.*

LAW & ORDER

I have already made my view clear to the court that I cannot and will not reveal the identity of my source and, therefore, I am faced ultimately with the threat of a contempt hearing and punishment of imprisonment. *Ian Paisley Jnr on the INLA murder of Loyalist Billy Wright in the Maze prison.*

Murder most foul

These people have stepped outside the bounds of humanity, killing anyone that gets in their way. They will have to be taken out of society and if the Gardaí need more resources to do this then the Minister for Justice will just have to supply them. *Limerick Mayor John Gilligan on the murder of businessman Roy Collins.*

This legislation will allow the Gardaí to use surveillance devices to gather information about serious criminals and, crucially, it will permit the use in court of evidence gathered in this way. It is very difficult to expect ordinary citizens to have the courage to give evidence in the light of what has happened. *Minister for Defence Willie O'Dea.*

I didn't know what to do. I just held him and waited and waited. All he said to me was, 'I love you, Da, and tell mum I love her.' He was just worried that he was going to die. I told him he wasn't. I didn't think he was. *Roy Collins' father Stephen.*

There is often a Robin Hood element with some of these crime families. The local community know these people. They are not outsiders. There is often gift-giving to maintain the illusion that 'these are our people'. It happened with the Colombian mafia and I'd say it's happened in Limerick too. *Jonathan Culleton, Waterford Institute of Technology.*

Pig ignorance
We've the World Music Centre, the Irish Chamber Orchestra, the Hunt Museum. We have the biggest tag-rugby festival in Ireland, the Pig'n'Porter, with more than 1,600 participants ... it's horrendous that our city is being terrorised by a small minority of thugs. They're terrorists and they're all you hear about all the time from Limerick, the bad news. We have to make sure the good news is heard. *Laura Ryan, Limerick Co-Ordination Office.*

Slap in the face
The court did not consider the issue of physical punishment, in the main, due to a technicality in that I do not have what is called victim status. *Patricia Lewlsey, NI Commissioner for Children and Young People, abandons the attempt to have smacking banned.*

If the children's commissioner cannot act on behalf of all children, who can? *Progressive Unionist Party leader Dawn Purvis.*

Vested interest
In the past we've seen instances of escorts leaving courts or prisons where the prisoner has a bullet-proof vest, the Garda has a bullet-proof

vest and the prison officer is wearing a tie. For us this is unacceptable. We're entitled to the same protection as everybody else. *Jim Mitchell, Prison Officers' Association.*

FADÓ, FADÓ
In scale it is comparable, for example, to Croke Park's pitch. The Hill of Tara had enormous ritual significance over the course of 5,000–6,000 years, so it's not surprising that you get monuments of the scale of the ditch pit circle. *Dr Fenwick, Department of Archaeology, NUI Galway, on the discovery of a ditch circling the Mound of Hostages.*

Rubbish tip-off
It didn't mean a whole lot to me—it was a flat piece of gold and I didn't think anything of it. It wasn't something you could wear or make use of. It didn't excite me in any way because in those days no one had tuppence to rub together, so we had no jewellery of any sort at that stage. *Sunniva Sheehan, Strokestown, Co. Roscommon, on a pre-Christian gold lunula discovered with two sun discs by her father in 1947, subsequently stolen and discarded in a Dublin rubbish bin.*

It was spotlessly clean. It was glowing, it was so bright. If we had missed that then the contents of the bins would have gone to the main dump. It would be another thousand years before the collar was found again. *Detective Garda Noel Galvin, on its retrieval, following a tip-off by Sergeant John Costello.*

CALLS OF NATURE
I've never had anyone directly trying to stop me. Guerrilla gardening is questioning to a degree the concept of private property. Property is held up as being sacred. I believe that access to land is a fundamental human right. *John Baker, Rochestown, Cork, who has been planting in secret around the city.*

Tall story
There have been situations where someone in a remote area might have been the only person to have seen a tornado but has been reluctant to admit to it in case their family and friends would think they were mad. If more people know about their existence then the more likely it is that they will report them. *John Tyrell, Tornado Storm Research Organisation.*

Horse power
Some things don't add up with horses. Human beings don't control everything. There is a far greater power than what we can figure out. We are only programmed to understand so much. Yes, God. That's a power we can't understand. Sometimes there aren't logical reasons for things to happen with horses. We do things with horses that make no sense but they work for that horse. *Trainer Aidan O'Brien.*

China tea shop
I was serving a customer at the counter when I saw something going into the store. I didn't know what it was, so I went into the store after it. I was amazed when I went into the store and saw that it was a bull. I was reared on a farm, but I never expected to meet a bull in this environment. *Bernie Morrin, Cummins' Supervalu, Ballinrobe, Co. Mayo.*

MYLES AWAY
They have turned into a bicycle. *Labour's Michael D. Higgins explains the frequent absence of Green Party ministers at Dáil business sessions.*

You were beaten with a bamboo cane until you screamed

Paddy Doyle, abuse survivor and author of The God Squad, *remembers. Publication of the Ryan Report into institutions run by the religious orders prompts widespread horror, anger and disbelief, which reciprocal pious platitudes and apologies do nothing to assuage.*

Society at large remained completely indifferent to the violence, the slave labour, the starvation, so you were left to the mercy of the Brothers and the various gangs that roamed the yard. I want to see the United Nations called in to investigate how 150,000 people ended up in this system. *Author Mannix Flynn, incarcerated and abused in Letterfrack, 1968.*

I am particularly ashamed of the abuse that occurred in Letterfrack and Clifden. I ask forgiveness of those who suffered. Abuse of children when perpetrated by a priest or religious is both a terrible crime and a betrayal of sacred trust. *Michael Neary, Archbishop of Tuam.*

I had a vocation. Even after I was abused, I still had it, so I was thoroughly crushed when they told me I wasn't suitable. They knew Father Payne had abused me. He was suitable for the priesthood, but I was being told I wasn't. When we were growing up, God and the Catholic Church were one and the same. So in my mind, I decided that if they would rather Ivan Payne over me, I would have nothing to do with God or his Church ever again. *Survivor Andrew Madden.*

I think of those in religious orders and some of the clergy in Dublin who have to face these facts from their past, which instinctively and quite naturally they'd rather not look at. That takes courage, and we shouldn't forget that this account today will also overshadow all of the good that they also did. *Vincent Nichols, Archbishop of Westminster.*

First of all, Minister, you made a bags of it in the beginning by changing the judges. You made a complete bags of it at that time because I went to the Laffoy Commission and ye had seven barristers there questioning me, telling me that I was telling lies when I told them that I got raped of a Saturday, got an [un]merciful beating after it and he then came along the following morning and put Holy Communion in my mouth. You don't know what happened there. You haven't the foggiest. *Abuse survivor and former mayor of Clonmel Michael O'Brien confronts Noel Dempsey on 'Questions and Answers'.*

While it may appear that this report closes a long chapter by revealing a shameful past, today's continued failings show this is not the case. Recent events, such as those in Monageer, continue to demonstrate to us that inadequate State and societal responses continue to fail children. *Clíona Saidléar, Rape Crisis Network Ireland.*

I hate the bastards. *Gerry Kelly, abused in Artane.*

MAMMON
In bad times people realise that politics matters. During bad economic times, interest in politics increases and when times are good people don't realise politics is important. It is only when there is less money in their account that they realise that politicians directly affect them. *Dr Liam Weeks, University College Cork.*

Hard sell
There is little point in a business spending a lot of time selling to a customer who was going to buy a product anyway or to one who is never going to buy it. *Michael Keaney, SAS Ireland.*

PriceWatershedCoup
It's like Christmas Day. There's a bounce back in the streets here; it's like fair day in Ballycastle. *Bill Tosh, Dundalk Chamber of Commerce, on the effect of reduced prices in selected Tesco border stores.*

All new, dramatically lower prices will apply to all our stores—from Youghal to Dundalk. We are committed to our policy of 'One Country, One Price'. *Lidl spokeswoman Aoife Clark.*

Many of our people have gone up to Drogheda for a look and, while they don't feel the offer is as has been presented, they'll be watching to see how consumers respond. *Tara Buckley, RGDATA, the retail grocers' organisation.*

Eggstraordinary General Meeting
Have you any understanding, or comprehension, as a board, of the pain you've caused? The pain I can tell you is real; it's unbelievable, it's breathtaking and life-taking in some circumstances. I hope you, the board, will carry the burden of this pain for the rest of your life . . . *Shareholder Susan Kelly at Allied Irish Bank's EGM.*

If we didn't live in a tolerant society, the chairman and the rest of the board would be hanging by their necks with piano wire. *Shareholder Gary Keogh, subsequent to throwing eggs in anger at AIB chairman Dermot Gleeson.*

It's like a barrel of apples. Put ten bad apples into it and what do you get at the end of the year? A full barrel of rotten apples. *Shareholder Cornelius Cagney.*

Blue chip
If someone told me he was a billionaire, I'd drop dead or give him an extra bag of chips. *Takeaway restaurant worker Chrissie Travers, Goresbridge, Co. Kilkenny, casts doubts on the reputed wealth of neighbour Stuart Pearson.*

AN TEANGA BHEO
The Irish revel in words. The rhythm and structure we use is different to the way English is spoken in the UK—it's baroque, colourful, quirky, conversational. It can sometimes even seem illogical, but the sense emerges in an entertaining, roundabout way. *Novelist Marian Keyes.*

A lot of Irish literature comes from wonderful mistakes that happened between the Irish language and English language. And I think people incorporate these mistakes really well into their conversation. They're confident in them, whereas I feel I need to conquer the language and be very cautious about it. *Novelist Hugo Hamilton.*

Listen and learn

Yes, it is a landmark event. It enables us to listen to the concerns of the Irish-speaking community locally and to address those concerns. It is our responsibility to reach out to all communities and this is a simple part of that process. *Assistant Chief Constable Judith Gillespie on a Derry meeting of the NI Policing Board held primarily in Irish.*

Traditionally the Irish-language community and the police have not exactly engaged with one another, but this is a sign of how much progress has been made here. *Gearóid Ó hÉara, former Derry mayor.*

TRAFFIC & TRAVEL

Spitting is the worst. People driving by will spit on you out the window. Motorists that get a bit disgruntled after getting clamped— and we've seen them physically do this—actually urinate on the clamp. *David Spencer, Dublin Street Parking Services.*

Anti-social whirl

You have to be realistic. It's just too expensive to run a helicopter, now that business has contracted. We don't use it any more. Everyone has cut back. All helicopters are mothballed; all helicopters are in the hangars. It's too ostentatious to be flying around. I think to use one would be too much in people's faces, I really do. *TV3 'Apprentice' star Jackie Lavin.*

Of course I can manage without it. Helicopter travel to my mind is a luxury. It's doubtful if I would get one again ... If you need to know anything about helicopter use at the moment, all you need to do is listen to the sky. You can hear birds singing again. *Businessman Ben Dunne.*

Rule of thumbing

I was getting a lift in this car and we passed an old guy on the side of the road who was hitching with a fridge. It just struck me as very strange. I remember recounting what I'd seen a few weeks later to friends in a pub back home in Brighton and saying that if there was one country where you could hitch with a fridge, that was Ireland. *Comedian Tony Hawks.*

CÉAD MÍLE FÁILTE
The Celtic Tiger was no friend to tourism. We became too busy; tourism slid down the pecking order. Tourists were only getting in the way of us getting in the way of ourselves—whether it was roads, airports or public transport. We started losing the welcome. We were meeting customers who were saying, 'You're the first Irish we've met.' *Jim Deegan, Railtours Ireland.*

Fair city
I was canvassing on the North Circular Road when I approached two guys on the street and was about to introduce myself. Before I got the chance, one of them said, 'Get off this street. Black people make me sick.' Then the younger of the two men said, 'If you don't get off this street, I'll put a bullet in your head.' *Independent local election candidate Patrick Maphoso.*

Lodgeistics
The Boyne is hallowed ground as far as the Orange Order is concerned. We are delighted that we have been able to form a lodge which is literally based on the river bank. We really think it will enhance the tourist potential in the area, and we have been heartened by the local reaction. *Jack Leetch, deputy master elect, Boyne L.O.L. 1690.*

DE MORTUIS
David Marcus was an eminence in the lives of writers of my generation and after. In the late 1960s he brought to Dublin a whiff of the wider world of London and late Bloomsbury, which was something Dublin badly needed in those days. He had a peculiarly serene confidence that good writing would out, and a determination to help in that process. *Novelist John Banville. David Marcus died this month.*

He was a man of strong preferences, not always coinciding with mine (or anyone else's), not interested in safe choices either, but personally always gracious, interested especially in promoting the unknown, sometimes the unformed, writers of the future. *Poet Eiléan Ní Chuilleanáin.*

He was the keeper of the flame: David Marcus singlehandedly kept the Irish short story tradition alive, by supporting writers at home and advocating them abroad. He had, as an editor and a man, endless grace and good manners. *Novelist Anne Enright.*

Last September at his daughter's wedding, though already ill and genially lost to Alzheimer's, he read with astounding clarity, intelligence and love his poem 'The House of Love', for Sarah and Tom. It was a beautiful and moving moment. *Critic and editor Niall MacMonagle.*

PARTY LINES
We had been Fianna Fáil all our lives—my father, my grandfathers, you name it. I'm absolutely ashamed to think that we supported those people to do what they have done to us. It's a sad, sad situation. I was a person who obeyed the law. I was never in a courthouse until Shell brought me there. *Willie Corduff, Co. Mayo 'Shell to Sea' pipeline protestor.*

Few happy returns
I join with Deputy Kenny in marking the first anniversary of the Taoiseach's elevation to office . . . I hope there won't be a second one. *Labour leader Eamon Gilmore.*

Shakers and movers
I'd actually ask people to transfer to people who have a vision for Dublin as a vibrant, green, enterprising city. *Green Party minister Eamon Ryan.*

Yates' summer school
When Ivan Yates was young and inexperienced, and he was once, I persuaded him one night in a back room in Murphy Flood's Hotel in Enniscorthy that it would boost his political career if he was the minister who delivered a 'charter of farmers' rights'. Ivan never looked back, but the department never forgot or forgave the stroke. *Michael Berkery, retiring chief executive, Irish Farmers' Association.*

Propper order

If the DUP truly cared about thwarting Sinn Féin, they would not have advanced them to the heart and very top of government, nor split the vote in this election. You can't prop up Sinn Féin in government nine to five in Stormont and then go out, with credibility, at night to tell voters you are the party to stop the Shinners. *Traditional Unionist Voice leader Jim Allister.*

Fianna failing

This logo has been around since 1927. For good or ill, it's part of our national heritage. Today it seems to be on the verge of extinction. The Minister for the Environment obviously has too many problems of his own to cope with this crisis, so perhaps FF should ask An Taisce to step in. Remember we can keep the logo without having to keep the party. *Naas Labour councillor Paddy McNamara on the Cheshire-Cat-like fading of the Fianna Fáil logo from election posters.*

Disassembly

I have listened very carefully to numerous statements from both the DUP and the UUP and I really do see in this agenda an attempt being made to restore unionist majority rule in this assembly. *Deputy First Minister Martin McGuinness.*

I believe that the future of Northern Ireland rests very strongly in the development of the Northern Ireland Assembly and I have a commitment to that Assembly to make sure that it works. *First Minister Peter Robinson.*

Taking the plunge

It's like going to the top of a big diving board. When you look at it from down below and say, 'I'm going to jump off that,' you think, 'Oh God, no!'—and you get the willies. Now I've jumped and I'm in that great big pool, but I have no idea what's underneath this water. I know people say I am mad. But maybe we need a bit of madness. *RTÉ's economics editor George Lee opts for Fine Gael candidacy.*

HIS & HERS

Making women feel deficient is something magazines do very well— in the 1950s the emphasis was on housekeeping skills, today it's breast size or wrinkle count. Magazines are the outer manifestation of the carping inner critic that resides in every female. *Writer Orna Ross.*

Bachelor has-beens

I have seen the term 'confirmed bachelor' written about me. The term 'eligible bachelor' means a great catch, form an orderly queue, ladies. 'Confirmed bachelor' means don't bother queuing, ladies, because you will be out all night and when you get to the till all the goods will be gone. *'VIP' magazine publisher Michael O'Doherty.*

First lady

There has never been a woman in the history of the State in this area that has run for local government and that raises big issues with me; do I buy into what's there or do I try and change it? *Rose Conway Walsh plans an assault on Mayo County Council.*

First person singular

I am not married, my father was an only child, my mother was an only child, and I was their only child. So things I might tell a sibling or a wife I tell my close friends. It can be tough to be unmarried, especially in rural Ireland, where the marriage culture has traditionally been strong. *RTÉ sportscaster Marty Morrissey.*

Mum's Army

It will be very hard leaving family behind, but leaving home is very much part of the job. I am very proud to be the first woman to act as deputy commander, and especially when it is the Western brigade, as I am from Galway. *Chad-bound Commandant Maureen O'Brien, appointed the first female deputy commander of an overseas unit.*

I understand that towards the end of pregnancy, women must wear civilian clothes as they cannot wear a uniform. It should be a very simple matter to design a uniform to accommodate these people. *Jimmy Deenihan TD.*

Meeow

My problem is that I have no idea what her policies are. Election literature came through the door from all the candidates. Her only platform appears to be that she was a Fianna Fáil president's daughter.

I think she's a Foxrock girl who was a former Green Party councillor who is now on the Labour ticket in a different constituency where she doesn't live. *Retiring MEP Avril Doyle on aspirant MEP Nessa Childers.*

I would be quite honest and say I don't have a huge knowledge about agriculture. *Nessa Childers.*

LAW & DISORDER
I'm going back to prison and, you know, apart from the upset to my family, I don't really care. You think about things a lot when you're inside and get your priorities straight. I can't deny that I'm dis-appointed with the way the INLA has handled things but at the same time I'm not going to get into a sniping match with them. What's hap-pened has happened. That's me finished with the INLA and done with Dublin. As soon as I get out I'm taking my family back to Armagh. *Declan 'Whacker' Duffy, charged with membership of an illegal organisation.*

No light on the subject
So far we have been unable to substantiate his claims concerning alleged costs of €1,100 to replace three bulbs in an unnamed Garda station. Despite repeated requests to name this station by the OPW, and indeed members of the media, Mr O'Boyce has so far declined to do so. *Minister of State Martin Mansergh.*

Frank appraisal
He has suffered enormously. I'm aware for some people he couldn't suffer enough, but he has visited a life sentence upon himself. *Colm Allen SC, erstwhile counsel for Frank Dunlop, who pleaded guilty to bribery charges.*

The word must go out from this court that the corruption of politicians, or anyone in public life, must attract significant penalties. *Judge Frank O'Donnell to Dunlop before imposing a custodial sentence.*

Dog daze
I've heard instances in Clare where criminals, knowing there was a guard dog, would bring in a bitch in heat and leave her off. A boxer is a big enough dog, but sedatives can knock out even the biggest dog cold in just a few minutes. *Noel Shinnors, Limerick Society for the Prevention of Cruelty to Animals.*

ARTS & PARTS

I absolutely hate political journalists. I think they are fucking arseholes. Their egos are bigger than the people they are dealing with. They think what they do is incredibly important, when all it is is just gossip. Their sense of humour is the sort they would have in the bar after they have been in the Dáil. All in-jokes. *Comedian Colin Murphy.*

Earning his stripes

People always talk about how difficult it is to get a first novel published, but it's very difficult to sustain a career in literary fiction if you're not having hits. I've seen so many people get dropped, friends of mine, who maybe published one or two books and it's all over before they're even 30, and it's devastating. And I could see that happening to me. I mean, it was happening to me. *John Boyne, author of* The Boy in the Striped Pyjamas.

Hear, hear

When a child is learning classical music, they learn to read music straight away. Which is a pity, because they become totally reliant on the written notes, whereas essentially music is aural. Somehow or other, it doesn't allow at least some of them to develop their ear, and their confidence to learn without reading the notes. *Traditional musician Máirtín O'Connor.*

Back to the wall

I believe, and hope, they will always be present. They are part of our tradition, which is unique to Belfast. Because of that, it should be preserved and encouraged. Rather than showing who's in control or for propaganda purposes, they're used for heralding heroes like George Best. Murals have diversified a great deal. *Mark Ervine, mural painter and son of the late Progressive Unionist Party leader.*

Undress code

There's a common misconception about burlesque. People often straight away think 'stripper' or 'nipple tassels'. But you don't have to get down to your underwear to do a burlesque show. It's not at all like that. *Burlesque promoter Lauren Murphy.*

Hallmarked

Cecil Day-Lewis said that the enemy of good art was the pram in the hall. But look what was in that pram—Daniel Day-Lewis. *Actor Dominic West.*

'ATIN' & DRINKIN'

Being a Guinness taster sounds like the ideal job, but it can be exhaustingly hard work. They spend three intense hours concentrating and analysing 30 different attributes of beers and then scoring them between zero and 100. *Guinness chemist David Jackson.*

Conic sections

Eating an ice cream is an experience that everyone does differently. Some people like the cone; some people like the ice cream. Some people work really hard at making sure that ice cream lasts right down until the end of the cone. I'd be one of them. I can't stand when I get half-way down the cone and the ice cream has run out. You cheat a little bit; you press it down with your tongue to make sure it's right there until the very end. *Journalist John Waters.*

Hospitalitea

Chinese people like to have some familiar dishes available on their trips abroad—noodle and rice dishes, seafood, light soups, fresh fruit, etc. Hot food at breakfast is common but not exactly an Irish breakfast—rice porridge, hot rolls or even stir-fry is a typical Chinese breakfast. It would be a good idea to provide green tea as well as the more traditional Irish cuppa. *Susan Li, chief Chinese representative, Tourism Ireland.*

Source for the goose

People watch them on TV and food fads change accordingly. If a cook on a Saturday morning programme uses lamb shanks you'll know within a couple of hours! A few years ago, when a programme a few days before Christmas recommended goose fat for roast potatoes, I lost count of the number of people who came looking for goose fat. *Rathmines, Dublin butcher David Nolan.*

Go figgure

We'll take that with us to our grave. *As the Tallaght factory closes, third-generation Jacob's employee Maria Breen refuses to reveal the secret of how Jacob's get the figs into the Fig Rolls.*

ONLY A GAME

I hope that in respect of other valuable debates and innovations that are conceptualised in this house, the media will cover them in the appropriate fashion, and not just in a demeaning way, such as how it was suggested we did not sit yesterday because of golf. *Senator Marc McSharry protests at media reports that the Seanad did not sit as a consequence of an Oireachtas Golf Society outing.*

Far foreign fields

The reality in Chad is that the ground is very hard. Some of the sports are played out on open ground and when people fall it tends to have a much greater impact on their bodies than falling in a field in Ireland, where the ground is not nearly as hard. *Defence minister Willie O'Dea explains why soccer and volleyball are denied to the Irish UN forces.*

Rock and a hard place

Would he ever just miss? He already has the half million. *Shane Lowry on his way to defeating Robert Rock in the playoff for the Irish Open golf championship. As an amateur he cannot collect the prize money of €500,000.*

Shakespeare, James Joyce, Brendan Behan, Seán O'Casey—they've all had a go at writing a few yarns, but I don't know if they've ever written anything as unbelievable as what we've witnessed over the last few hours. *Irish Open commentator Con Murphy.*

Counter culture

The biggest single most difficult issue we face is under-the-counter payments. There is a well-known mercenary manager being paid by two very well-known businessmen, fanatical GAA followers. *GAA director general Paraic Duffy.*

Best foot backward

When you win something, a lot of players take stock and all of a sudden you use it as a platform to get better, to move forward. And sometimes to get better and move forward you work on your weaknesses . . . and when you work on your weaknesses, sometimes your strengths get a little weak . . . Because I've been so focused on working on things, my strengths have definitely not been as good. So, like a lot of things, if you're trying to move forward, you often have to take a step back. *Champion golfer Pádraig Harrington.*

Testicle match

Arsenal Ladies have won the league—credit to them for showing more balls than their male counterparts. *Former Republic of Ireland soccer player Tony Cascarino.*

SOCIAL & PERSONAL

I believe deeply that the two systems that held Irish society for generations were the family and community, and both of them were being seriously disrupted. We weren't going to get factories in the Feakles of this world so I got the idea that if I could get something going to build houses, young couples, instead of moving to Limerick or Shannon or Ennis, young native people could buy their own house in Feakle. I started there, I got the local bank manager, three or four other people, we bought a site and we built 20 houses and we got 20 young families to live in Feakle. *Retiring Rural Housing Organisation founder Fr Harry Bohan.*

Vanishing Irish

Ireland, and Dublin particularly, is a great place to disappear. It's a real melting pot of cultures so it's easy to blend in. It's not too difficult for people to acclimatise and it's not too expensive. Also, it's quite a safe place on the scale of things. We can't guarantee anything. But no one I've helped disappear has ever been found. *New Yorker and former 'skip tracer' Frank M. Ahearn.*

We've helped people again and again to find their families and reunite with them. It's an area that a lot of people wouldn't know about, but when you see the difference it makes to people's lives, it really is quite beautiful. *John Roycroft, Irish Red Cross.*

Space invaders

Italians are an intriguing race. They are always trying to feed you and hug you and kiss you but take someone's parking space and they'd shoot you. They're like the Irish when we've had a few drinks on us, except they haven't had the drink. *Novelist Christine Dwyer Hickey.*

Losing the head

I think people in Ireland don't take care for their headspace at all. They regard it as self-indulgent. If you have a problem in Ireland, you drink your face off. Whereas at least in New York, there's decades of an attitude of trying to take care of your mind. People in Ireland go, 'What would you want with that fucking therapy stuff?' *Writer/ performer Mario Rosenstock.*

FAITH & MORALS

You hear politicians hopping on the anti-Catholic Church. I think that's sad. Most of them were educated by the Catholic Church, and now here they are just jumping at it and running around wanting to sell Catholic schools and churches. *Former Taoiseach Bertie Ahern.*

Three days' wonder

Last Wednesday I celebrated Mass in Arbour Hill, Dublin, and blessed the graves of executed 1916 leaders. Tomorrow, I hope to preach at the service of thanksgiving and commemoration in the College Chapel of Trinity College Dublin. Today, I am here at the Eucharist to mark the closure of the Church of Ireland Synod. To some people, all of that seems an impossible combination. But what it does suggest, perhaps, is that we live in remarkable times. *Cardinal Seán Brady.*

Extra mural

My sister lives opposite a derelict house, and the sun was setting when she looked out her window and saw an image on the gable wall. She asked our mam to look without telling her what she had seen, and did the same with my father. They all saw what seems to be an image of Our Lord with a cross to the right-hand side. *Donna Delaney, Ballina, Co. Mayo.*

Credulous and sometimes pious people seem to be more susceptible to such imaginings, but imaginings they are. A characteristic, too, is that people undergoing some kind of trauma or caught in the slipstream of other people's trauma can more easily imagine signs and messages. Invariably, after a few weeks and all of the excitement, it becomes no more than a memory. *Ballina parish priest Fr Brendan Hoban.*

CALLS OF NATURE
He's in with the chickens but he thinks he's a Bernese mountain dog. He latched onto our dog at home and thought she was his mother. *At Donabate's Petting Zoo, comedian Brendan O'Carroll's pet duck undergoes an identity crisis.*

Gorilla tactics
We were planning a wonderful rainforest project for our gorillas. We had hoped to start building it this September and have it ready for next spring. We may have to delay that project now. *Dublin Zoo director Leo Oosterweghel laments budget cuts.*

Plots thicken
My grandfather had an allotment in Inchicore, only it wasn't called that then—people would talk about 'plots'. It's great to see that practice coming back. There are even some farmers giving over plots of land near urban areas, where formerly it was only the local authority who provided gardening sites. *Bloom project manager Gary Graham.*

Those were the daisies
There are 1,000 people a week on the mountain these days and on any given Sunday as many as 300 will be climbing the mountain. What we are seeing now is the most famous route onto our highest mountain washed away literally before our eyes. There were daisies growing on the Devil's Ladder 30 years ago. Now all we have is a sluice of mud and scree. *Carrántuathail guide Con Moriarty.*

Mud larks
Winter is our busiest season. We have massive drainage in the trails, so it never gets too wet, but I think people actually like mountain biking for the opportunity it gives them to get mucky. I think it brings out everyone's inner child. They come back in at 4 p.m. covered from

head to toe with mud and grinning from ear to ear. *Chris O'Callaghan, Cross Country Trails.*

It's not too bad in the past five years after we got a harvester, but before that I used to get up at 6.30 a.m. every morning, load up lads in the jeep and go off. They'd get out to pick the parsnips on a wet morning and they'd be stuck in the muck trying to pull parsnips. One lad said to me, 'You'd be better off doing time in the Joy. Hard labour wouldn't be as hard as this.' *Fingal farmer Matt Thorne.*

Graze and favour
When the cows were first introduced to the site, it was overgrown, but now with the cows manicuring the site, it has shown how essential cows are to the Burren. What is happening at Poulnabrone is a model for the rest of the Burren. *Farmer Pat Nagle's cattle help conserve the 5,800-year-old dolmen.*

Dung deal
I, more than anyone, want dung removed from roads in Killarney National Park, for the benefit of parents, children and other visitors ... I will accept the expertise of those who have been driving horses for as many as 46 years before accepting the opinions of the Minister's staff, who have probably never been on a horse. *Tom Sheahan TD.*

The sheep and the ghosts
Farmers cannot get burial licences, but must go to the vet. It's a disaster that will come back to haunt you. *Willie Penrose TD on the cut in the Fallen Animal Scheme.*

LAST ORDERS
I asked her for a pint of Harp and a packet of crisps. *Grand Slam and Ulster rugby flanker Stephen Ferris meets Queen Elizabeth II.*

June 2009

A whiff of political decay and rotting greens

assails the nasal sensibilities of Fine Gael's Alan Shatter following what is, for the Government parties, the discouraging result of the local and European elections. Ryan reverberates. Irish and British Lions go south. Cliché of the Month: 'tsunami'—especially uttered minus the 't'.

You can be a non-politician coming into an election, but you are never a non-politician after that . . . I hope George Lee will be a little more than a lightning rod for people's anger. *Dublin South Labour candidate Alex White.*

Looks like he'll be assumed into heaven before noon. *Former Labour leader Pat Rabbitte on novice Fine Gael candidate Lee.*

Politicians go around grabbing people's hands and imposing themselves on reluctant bystanders. Babies also have a civil right not to be kissed by every passing politician. *Labour MEP candidate Joe Higgins.*

I am one of the lucky ones. I got the vote of the people. At this stage I am very, very angry. I have to get the full list of casualties. We lost a lot of good people, a lot of them good friends of mine, who never did anything wrong. I think there will be recriminations. *Arthur McDonald, Fianna Fáil national councillors' organisation.*

This is not a good day for Fianna Fáil in electoral terms. *Minister for Foreign Affairs Micheál Martin.*

RYAN AIRED

In the midst of a national trauma, there have been too many impetuous responses without the humility of sufficient pause for thought and reflection. Many of these are tangential to the needs of the victims; all other agendas should be set aside. Some people in Ireland have used this report as a springboard towards a secularising agenda. *Paul Colton, Bishop of Cork, Cloyne and Ross.*

I benefited from a good education by the Christian Brothers. Most fair-minded people would acknowledge that the vast majority of the religious who taught in our schools were not involved in abuse. However, I was appalled at the attitude taken by the representatives of the congregations when I met them in December 2003 to request that they pay the State the €6 million they received from their insurance companies as an *ex gratia* payment. I told the congregations they had a moral obligation to hand over this money. We subsequently repeated the request twice in writing but were refused on both occasions. *Minister for Transport Noel Dempsey.*

Ours is not a country of dancing leprechauns, shared laughter and thousands of smiles. This story is our genocide. It is no different from the 1890 story of Indians in Canada, where 50,000 kids died in institutions. *Damien Moore, seven years in St Vincent's Orphanage, Glasnevin, Dublin.*

I came up to Dublin today because I feel very strongly about this. You see the walking wounded in the town, who suffered abuse and it was never dealt with. The number talking about abuse in day schools on the march here today is just phenomenal. *Laurie Ennis, Portarlington.*

This was our mini-Holocaust. The Government and religious tried to pretend we were not hurt in these institutions. We were not criminals! *Marcher Marie Therese O'Loughlin, former resident of Goldenbridge.*

We have been silenced for so long, I wish we could do this 365 days a year. This is the survivors' Ascension Day. *Christine Buckley, director, Aislinn Centre.*

DE MORTUIS
The name Vincent O'Brien seemed not merely synonymous with horse-racing but its very embodiment and definition so that, now that he has gone, it is almost as if racing itself has died. *Fr Bruce Bradley sj at the thanksgiving Mass. Trainer Vincent O'Brien died this month at 92.*

Everything he did was geared to keeping his horses happy and relaxed at home so that they would perform to their full potential on the racecourse, and the results speak for themselves. There's really no argument: Vincent was the greatest. *Jockey Lester Piggott.*

He never dwelt on what went before. He wasn't into going over past glories. Tomorrow was what mattered. His motto was never to stop learning ... and never be content with second best. *Vincent's son Charles.*

As for so many people in racing, he was my hero growing up. There is nothing that compares to Ballydoyle anywhere in the world. I feel a sense of history every morning when I walk into a yard that has had horses such as Nijinsky, Sir Ivor and Sadler's Wells in it. It is humbling to follow in his footsteps. *Trainer Aidan O'Brien.*

HIS & HERS
I was talking to one woman about how we need change. She said, 'Don't worry, I'll drag you up them stairs and I'll change you.' *Local election candidate Seaghan Kearney on his reception on the doorsteps.*

Centres of attraction
There are quite a lot of strange people out there, though. They treat dating like a chocolate box in terms of picking and choosing. Men and women are so different in what they look for. The single white male is generally looking for something different to the single white female. Men want to go 10 years younger and want someone attractive and are quite specific about build. But the joy of dealing with men is that men know what they want. *Patricia Farrell, Topmatch Ireland.*

Well, in Ireland, there's so much more sidling up to people at parties and chatting them up than actual dating. I remember when I moved to New York, a man asked me out in the street and I was convinced he was a lunatic who had accosted me, until my American friends explained that it was normal. *Novelist Sarah Rees Brennan.*

Just a pretty face
I've had one or two people say, 'Jesus, you're a stunner,' or silly things like that, but it's great because it helps to strike up a conversation. *Labour election candidate Maria Parodi.*

I'm completely surprised by this level of interest. The day after the photographs came out, I got 800 emails. I even got a few marriage proposals. *Fine Gael election candidate Emma Kiernan features in photos on Facebook.*

Love of mic
There is no visual distraction. From my point of view as a female presenter, I find that very liberating. All research shows that if you are a woman on TV, people spend the first five minutes either praising or criticising what the presenter is wearing. *Miriam O'Callaghan prefers working in radio.*

Gentlemen pick knickers
Men are much more sophisticated buyers than they used to be back in the days when we first opened, when it seemed it was only men with mistresses who bought luxury lingerie and then it was very obviously sexy. Men have great taste and they put a lot of thought into what they buy. *Lingerie purveyor Susan Hunter.*

Sisters under the skin
People have an idea of what a Trinity student looks like, and an idea of what Page Three girls look like. Put the two together and they find it hard to reconcile. *Student model Claire Tully.*

Closed profession
Who are these men who think it's okay to pay for sex? Sex cannot be purchased. It must be negotiated between two consenting adults . . . this is not a career that any woman would choose if she could live an economically viable life another way. For which woman is it an okay career option? Not for my daughter. Not for your daughter. Whose daughter is it okay for? *Gráinne Healy, European Women's Lobby Observatory Organisation on Violence Against Women.*

He said she said
Seán once said to me, 'Of course you think I'm a shit, don't you?' I said, 'Yes, you are a bit of a shit—perhaps a nice shit.' But I didn't say it with any venom. I said, 'Ok, so what's new?' *Novelist Julia O'Faolain on her writer father's sexual dalliances.*

FAITH & MORALS

It's no harm if these religious orders are disbanded. Absolutely. Life is too short and precious. A life of love and companionship and teamwork—my idea is that we're bound together no matter what our religious background, if we can share a love of human rights and dignity, and a basic compassion for the poor and the sick. We can cross all barriers. I'm an unpaid volunteer. I like to tell my superiors, 'You don't own me.' *Fr Shay Cullen, Columban missionary in the Philippines.*

Holy ground

It is a rigmarole, it means nothing, and we should be alert to the fact that there are atheists, agnostics, Jews and Muslims, and I just think it makes a mockery of the whole thing, to invoke Jesus Christ as the source of our doings here. *Senator David Norris deplores the fact that Seanad sittings open with a prayer.*

Sinthesis

Greed is a problem. It knocked on our door and we welcomed it in, from bricklayers who charged €1.45 to lay a brick, to the big developer. That is capitalism. But I think that greed is an unfortunate aspect of it. *Solicitor Gerald Kean.*

TEANGA BHEO

There's a sense, sometimes, that people don't want to speak Irish. But they want all of the benefits that come with living in a Gaeltacht. You can't have it both ways. *Pádraig Gerriter, school principal, Daingean Uí Chúis.*

Tongue tide

We have pupils coming to us who do not speak English at all. They could be involved with four languages. For example, a pupil from Pakistan might have spoken Urdu in his country. At school he or she will be learning English, Irish and Arabic. We teach Arabic because it is the language of the Koran. *Colm McGlade, principal, Muslim National School, Clonskeagh, Dublin.*

I would like to stay in Ireland if possible. I find the people here open-minded and friendly. I speak Slovak, Czech, Polish, Russian, English and Hungarian, my mother's language. Since the recession came, a lot of people are not needed here any more, so I've also got to ask myself, 'Am I needed here or not?' *Slovakian Henrieta Porubecova.*

Both your houses

It is just a language—you can curse the Pope in Irish just as easily as you can curse the Queen in English. *Language consultant and former Belfast* News Letter *journalist Ian Malcolm, encouraging Protestants and Unionists to embrace the language.*

MAMMON

There are members of my congregation with modest savings and modest redundancy payments who have put them all in the PMS. They are good people who have worked hard and given sacrificially for the benefit of their Church . . . We simply ask—are Irish Presbyterian savers the only ones to remain unprotected when the Presbyterian Mutual Society is caught up in the same financial hurricane which is affecting the rest of the financial world? *Presbyterian Moderator Dr Stafford Carson.*

Just stringing along

Where you have high taxes you can have a situation where people decide not to kill themselves working harder to earn more. They might decide they would be better off learning to play the guitar rather than earning more to pay more tax. Doing things other than earning money is not necessarily a bad thing, but increased personal taxes can lead to a dampening of entrepreneurial activity. *Mike Gaffney,* KPMG.

Silence in court

Having got the legal advice, which we have to act upon, we gave the judges the opportunity to voluntarily give something to contribute to the present economic crises, and so far only one in 10 have done so, and I think that's a very poor example. *Minister Willie O'Dea.*

It's quite obvious that any appeal to their patriotism has met with a resounding silence to date. People in the public service who have been forced to pay this levy will be horrified and appalled. *Joe Behan TD.*

Unfair and misleading statements have been made concerning the position of the judiciary such as to the effect that all those who have not yet made a voluntary contribution have refused to do so. *Chief Justice John Murray.*

Divine afflatus
The boom did this at least: it took away our fatalism. We know now that there's no God up there wanting the Irish to be poor, just maybe a little less greedy. *Journalist Olivia O'Leary.*

CÉAD MÍLE FÁILTE
As a foreigner, the more the prosperity kicked in, the more invisible I felt I became. In 1995, when I first arrived, I felt like a curiosity, exotic, warmly welcomed, and this continued through 1996, 1997. But by 2000 things that hadn't happened to me in the beginning were starting to happen, like being called a 'fucking foreigner'. And now, it seems to me we are back at the softer Ireland that I first encountered. Friendlier, where people talk again, without the hysterical con-sumerism, which was just ridiculous. *Zlata Filipovi, writer.*

Ulster fright
They made signs like they wanted to cut my brother's baby's throat. They said they wanted to kill us. *Romanian Couaccusil Filius, following racist attacks in Belfast.*

They have no jobs, no homes, no money. They feel they may as well go home. Their families back home in Romania have heard all the media reports about what happened in Belfast and are frightened for them; they want them back home. *Assembly member Anna Lo.*

It is a symbol of the sectarianism that still divides us and it is a marker that the only way forward is a shared future. I am very disappointed that all but two of the Romanians have chosen to leave. *Social Development Minister Margaret Ritchie.*

Amazing race
I think I want to move to Ireland. It is always sunny (at least when we were there). The golf is amazing. The people couldn't be nicer. You can get a pint of beer just about anywhere you turn and all we did was

win races when we were there. And people wanted us to sign autographs and take photos with them all hours of the day. Hmmmm. What's not to like about that? *Volvo Ocean Race skipper Kenny Read,* US Puma, *reflects on his Galway landfall.*

LESSER BREEDS
Snakes are not native to Ireland so they could not be capable of surviving in the wild. These creatures would be vulnerable if out in the wild and, even though snakes sold in Ireland are not venomous, they are territorially narky creatures who are capable of biting. *Orla Aungier, Dublin Society for the Prevention of Cruelty to Animals, on escaped reptiles.*

Fur and feather
We are seeing species that have never been seen before in Ireland being introduced by these people. Look at the pine marten, the most nasty, vicious bird that you have ever seen. They were never in Ireland but have been introduced. *Former Westmeath councillor Michael Newman objects to the creation of special protection areas by the wildlife authorities.*

Extended paws
Fewer people used to have cars and they would go to great lengths to get their pet to us; they still do—they'll get time off from work or leave early. People really care. I saw a very serious alcoholic who didn't drink for four days because he wanted to be awake for the clinic in Donneycarney; no one else could stop him drinking, but the dog stopped him drinking . . . *Aidan Bailey, Blue Cross.*

PARTY LINES
The Republic is engaged in a major struggle to maintain, within the EU and indeed the euro zone, its economic viability and sovereignty. It is hardly the moment to press claims to the North which we have renounced, and it has to be said, the advantages and flexibility of joining up with a small sovereign state in the present global turmoil are for the moment a lot less compelling today than they were two or three years ago. *Minister of State Martin Mansergh.*

Dese don't doze

Members here may be in meditation; they may have their eyes closed or their heads down. They're meditating, they're contemplating, but I have never seen a member from any side of the house deep in sleep. *Leas-Cheann Comhairle Noel O'Flynn.*

That would be felling

All you have to do is look at the simple improbability of his biography and at the suggestions that he was, at 20, 22 years of age, running the largest forestry operation in the former Soviet Union. You just have to look at any of these so-called facts and you could begin to ask serious questions. *Minister for European Affairs Dick Roche on Libertas leader Declan Ganley.*

Farewell to arms

The IRA dealt with the issue of arms in a decisive way four years ago. If these reports prove to be true and the UVF have now followed suit then that would obviously be a welcome move. It is also important that other armed organisations go down this road. *Sinn Féin junior minister Gerry Kelly.*

If these reports were to be confirmed, what we would see would be a seismic transformation within loyalism. *Northern Secretary Shaun Woodward.*

HERE & THERE

He was able to crawl into some ruins, and lay there bleeding. Eventually, he heard an American member of the international brigade outside calling out, 'Are there any Americans here?' My father called back, 'No, but there is an Irishman here.' The American carried him through the streets to safety under sniper fire and my father was eventually treated. *Daughter Karen on Spanish Civil War veteran Paddy Cochrane, wounded in the battle of Belchite and now awarded Spanish citizenship.*

Fun of the Faroes

They say the Irish monks came here but judging by the—how do I say it?—very Irish looks of the people they didn't spend all their time praying. Very similar traits . . . sometimes I'd be standing around watching a game and they talk to me in Faroese because they think I'm one of them. *Faroe Islands national soccer manager Brian Kerr.*

Tara minefield

It's the curse of Tara. They've gone past the Mound of the Sages on Rath Lugh. I knew this would happen. *Emma Sharma-Hayes, Save Tara Campaign, on the devastation of the Government parties' election vote.*

Slaneway

On the laneway through the woods, we were stuck, squished together like cattle for two-and-a-half hours with metal fences either side of us. Some people were so wasted they were being sick on themselves, fights were breaking out and people were so drunk they could not stand up. There was no way to escape if there had been an emergency . . . *Sarah Milligan, London, attempts to return from the Oasis concert at Slane Castle.*

In the end we had to beg a taxi driver and pay way over the odds to get a lift. On the road we passed thousands of stranded people, many lying in ditches, many crying, many looking scared and lost and with no idea of where to go or how to get home. It was a surreal, frightening and horrible experience. *Dubliner Den Loughran.*

I'm very angry and upset about what's happened—from the problems in the laneway on the Dublin side to the difficulties that many people had getting home. *Lord Henry Mountcharles, Slane Castle.*

Exit strategy

Some nights at the Ivy were mayhem. You'd have chauffeur cars all the way up the road, you'd have 12 or 13 paparazzi out front, you'd have a restaurant full of celebrities. I'd have slipped somebody out the back door, avoided a punch and avoided getting a ticket. I'd go home and think, 'It's not a bad old job.' *Seán McDermott, Cappawhite, Co. Tipperary, doyen of London doormen.*

Buylocation

Worldwide, once you are inside an IKEA store you don't know which part of the world you're in. Once we are open, you will think you are in Belfast. *Dublin store manager Garry Deakin.*

BRICKS & MORTAR

There's building and there's architecture. Buildings just keep out the rain, but architecture means something more to society because of its lasting value. Architecture is a belief in the future, satisfying a need for shelter but also for continuity. It's only when you see places that have been blitzed or obliterated that you realise that fully. *Yvonne Farrell, Grafton Architects.*

Plumb crazy

There is certainly an increase in people trying to do it themselves. There are some things you just can't mess around with. A lot of people try to fix things and make a mess of it and finally back off, hands up. People sometimes go to an awful lot of expense trying to fix things themselves, and at the end of the day they just have to call the right guy. *Dublin plumber Tom Mullen.*

Sails pitch

Windmill has been dormant for such a long time that we think it'll rejuvenate the industry to have it up and running again. When we first came in, you could actually feel the cold and the lack of love in the building, and it's a matter of getting Windmill back to its 1980s' heyday. *Naomi Moore, one of the three new owners of the former U2 studios.*

SOCIAL & PERSONAL

Happiness is the freedom of diving through the invisible line where crystal-clear aquamarine water meets the air. It is an almost imperceptible transition into a different realm where one is observed by the passing dogfish or conger eel. *Artist Dorothy Cross.*

Dermotology

It's a job. Well, I am where I am. It's very hard to get out of politics once you're in it, even if you wanted to get out. There is an element of loyalty, and ultimately there's an element that it puts bread on the table. I would have to find a job elsewhere, and it's probably a bit difficult nowadays. *Minister for Justice Dermot Ahern.*

Means to an end

You're quite philosophical about it and then suddenly as you keep thinking like this, the actual prospect of doing it becomes more amenable. And you know, maybe it's not such a bad idea any more and you don't think about 'dead, six feet under, funeral, parents grieving'. That stuff doesn't go through your head. *Sports commentator George Hook on contemplating suicide.*

Ringing the changes
For many years the phone box was at the centre of Irish life. It was our connection to the outside world and we used it for so many purposes. Sadly, though, the time of the phone box has passed due to the advent of house phones, mobile phones and email, and as eircom rolls out its plan to remove many of the kiosks they are quickly disappearing from the landscape. *Aideen O'Sullivan plans a documentary to mark the disconnection.*

Unbelted earl
At Trinity I got a hard time from a couple of people and in a way I then realised we are what we are and there's no point hiding behind something we're not. I don't go around using the title every day. I don't introduce myself as . . . I'm just Alex Mountcharles at the end of the day. *Earl of Mountcharles.*

ARTS & PARTS
When we look back to the origins of the state, to the 1916 Proclamation, that rebellion was a work of art. As a military rebellion it was a disaster, but they were primarily artists making statements. They knew the value of symbols. What seemed to happen was that people like Pearse, MacDonagh (minor writers with a revolutionary aspiration) and people like Yeats (major artists with a minor interest in politics) looked at our past and our cultural inheritance, and they invented this idea. *Film-maker Alan Gilsenan.*

Top billing
From a practical point of view it's been a challenge to get the set in place. It had to be built and assembled off site, then broken down into small pieces—pieces that would fit in a lift—and re-assembled in the Vertigo Suite, some 17 storeys up. Getting 200 people up and down for the two shows each night presents its own problems . . . *Corcadorca artistic director Pat Kiernan on producing MedEia—a version of the original by Euripides—in Cork's tallest building.*

The bare thing

It was a very euphoric sort of moment where people celebrated the shared humanity of the naked body, because very often the only photographs we see of large groups of people naked are photographs of famine victims or of people in concentration camps. *William Galinsky, director, Cork Midsummer Festival, on the 1,100-odd people who stripped for us photo artist Spencer Tunick at last year's event.*

Here I am. I'm old and I'm naked, but I'm alive. *Nell McCafferty on her nude portrait by Daniel Duffy.*

Cause for rejoycing

It's wonderful to see literature taking over the city and there are lots of ordinary people, not just scholars. That's a very Joycean act. Yes, he's difficult and demanding to read, but look around you, and see how people have responded to him. That's what happens when you capture the soul of a people. *Novelist and translator Eduardo Lago celebrates Bloomsday.*

Closed book

I often think when I'm in the middle of a book, 'Does the world really need another book?', and very often the answer is 'No, it doesn't'. *Novelist John MacKenna.*

Anything I have had to say I have said it while in uniform. I have made my points. I have sent to Europe somewhere in the region of 226 recommendations about lessons identified and possibilities of what we might do. That's between me and those people. If they want to act on it, good enough. I will not be writing any book. *Retiring Lieut.-General Pat Nash, awarded the Légion d'Honneur in recognition of his peacekeeping work in Chad.*

De udder brudder

He tried to take advantage of the fact that Eric would not know who he was meeting, and yet he managed to get a photograph of his brother so his brother could bask in the reflected glory of Eric Cantona. I just thought it was cheap and I hope people saw through it. *Director Ken Loach disapproves of Bertie Ahern's presence at the premiere of* Looking for Eric. *(The brother was a local election candidate.)*

The higher a monkey climbs into the tree, the more you can see of its arse. *Looking for Eric film writer Paul Laverty.*

LAW & DISORDER
You didn't figure on people like us standing up and using all the resources of the law. What we have done here today is within the law. What the Real IRA did was outside the law and we have proven that, if the criminal justice system is not capable of delivering some justice, at least civil law is and that's a very strong message we send around the world. *Michael Gallagher, representative of the Omagh bombing victims, on the outcome of their civil action.*

Debterrent?
It's a bit outdated but imprisonment is the only consequence that consumer credit people can invoke. It is in nobody's interest that somebody goes to jail but there has to be a consequence. *Declan Flood, Irish Institute of Credit Management.*

The prison system and the courts system are being used in the course of a civil debt collection process, which means people end up in jail without ever committing even the smallest of offences ... There was a feeling that prison was a good thing because it forced people to pay their debts, but it doesn't. *Noeline Blackwell, Free Legal Advice Centres.*

Paper work
I want the people of Ireland to know how the 'Independent' media go about their business. They made up a story and for 4½ years they lied to the good people of Ireland about me. They took my reputation. They destroyed my business, and it has had a devastating effect on me and my family. *Communications consultant Monica Leech, awarded record damages for libel.*

ONLY A GAME
I would pick him because he is a special person. I mean I know he would die for you, so provided his body is okay and he got through the year I'd take him back in a heartbeat. *Sydney Swans coach Paul Roos on former player and Kerry footballer Tadhg Kennelly.*

Out with a bang

If you are going to participate in the Olympics you should be setting your targets high, and your mind should be focused enough to go for it. And then you work backwards from there. People are still struggling with that in this country; there's still this thing of, I suppose, 'Isn't it great just to get there?' The problem is, when you're there you're just cannon fodder. *Martin McElroy, Rowing Ireland.*

Runner being

Sonia is a runner's runner. She runs. That is what she does. She wins, she loses, she wins again. She has an almost mystical appreciation of the joy of running. *Iognáid Ó Muircheartaigh, president emeritus, NUI Galway, explains Sonia O'Sullivan.*

No Kingdom comeback

I was asked and I told them straight up I wasn't interested. I gave 38 years' service to Kerry as a player, selector, manager and what have you and I think 38 years is enough. They were wonderful but to tell the truth I've gotten more enjoyment in Kildare than anywhere. *Wicklow football manager Mick O'Dwyer.*

Moo-t point

The silage is cut and the cows will look after themselves. *Farmer and rugby player John Hayes, summoned to join the Lions team in South Africa.*

AN t-AOS ÓG

They decide to go backpacking around the world for six months and by the time they come home, having visited 12 countries, they don't know t'other from which. They haven't been there long enough, or quietly enough, to really take in the essence of the culture. They haven't read enough about the place before they've been there. *Author and traveller Dervla Murphy.*

Mind the gap

They're not getting any work experience; they can fall into bad habits and bad company and get into a habit of just being lazy. It's a disaster . . . it's not working at all in the way it was supposed to be. *Businessman Bill Cullen on the transition year.*

Crux and nannies

Nanny-sharing is certainly an area we're finding more demand for and expanding this year because of the way the economy has gone. It works out just slightly more expensive than a crèche, but it still means that parents can have their children looked after in familiar surroundings, and they're getting the kind of focused, expert attention that's so essential in their early years. *Carol Flynn, Nanny Solutions.*

Good things come in trees

I take city kids out exploring in the countryside and I remember one walking with his head turned up to the sky. He said he'd never dreamed of so many trees, and I guessed that most of the trees he'd occasionally see on his housing estate would be vandalised and broken. This was some kind of heaven for him. *Wicklow mountain guide Conny O'Connell.*

LAST POST

People don't pronounce rug as 'rueg' or hug as 'hueg', so why do they pronounce Bug as 'Bueg'? *Brendan Bugler, Clare hurler and non-musician, on the mispronunciation of his name.*

July 2009

I've been slapped with a plastic sword already

boasts 27-year-old Shirley Costelloe from Scariff, Co. Clare, attending Oxegen at Punchestown, Co. Kildare, for the first time and looking forward to seeing Florence and the Machine and Lady Gaga. 'The campsite usually resembles something like Calcutta,' says Sergeant Goode of Naas Garda Station: 'It takes us the guts of a week to sort through the lost property after the festival, but that's all part of the job.'

If you'd told me this time last year I'd be playing in front of 100,000 people I'd probably have told you to fuck off. *Lady Gaga.*

We try to educate people about composting toilets, but at Oxegen everyone is very young and very drunk so they don't give a stuff about the green aspect; they're here for the clean aspect. *Vix Jevons, Comfy Crappers.*

ARTS & PARTS

When you went in, there was an Irish flag on one side and the Cuban flag on the other side. It's very run-down, like an old warehouse. Very dusty, with a wooden floor and carcasses of pianos everywhere. There were maybe 15 pianos, everything from uprights to baby grands. We handed over the packages and they started opening them up there and then. One guy started shouting down to the back of the workshop to come and look at what was in the packages, so it must have been something he needed. *Catherine Bruton, Galway, delivers much-needed piano parts to Havana, on behalf of the Irish Una Corda project.*

Unfair city

I think Dublin was a very good training ground. It's a tough place. It's a really hard city. I had a play that was done in the Abbey and it failed. I was fired by Conor Brady off *The Irish Times*. I was a columnist and he dropped me. And that was not fun. And what I did was I went down to my then in-laws' cottage in West Cork and started my first book. *Novelist Douglas Kennedy.*

Resurrection man

We had to hide in the dark and pretend we were on a raft. Then we had to rise from the dead and run screaming at people and stop within an inch of their face, without hitting them. We then had to act as very intense zombies. I'm looking forward to hiding in the dark, jumping out and terrifying the life out of tourists. It beats sitting around in an office. *Corkonian and former archaeologist Jeremiah O'Connor signs up for the London Bridge Experience.*

In the round

Every village, every city, needs a theatre. It's not just a building; it's about being exposed to new ideas. Theatre changes the way we view society and connects us to global ideas. In the past, we've suffered from being closed off. *Actor Gabriel Byrne.*

End of story

I don't read her books. I've never read them. I read the first chapter but it wasn't my cup of tea. I said, 'Do you get away with that stuff?' and she said, 'That's light. Wait till you read the rest.' *Philip McLoughlin, partner of novelist Amanda Brunker.*

Food for thought

There was a farmer who used to come into the local pub with a lump of silage in his pocket. He'd sit there, chewing bits off the edge of it. People laughed at it, but they accepted it as well. I guess it's that idea of having no rules that I try to recreate in my stand-up comedy now. *Eleanor Tiernan.*

Pro Bono

I have a bank account specifically for u2. I put money in it each month and then I can use that to follow them wherever. It's my only hobby. I'm only going to two of the Croke Park gigs because we're going on a family holiday on Monday. *Therese van Roosmalen, Holland.*

Thanks to the GAA for the use of the hall. *Bono at Croker.*

'ATIN' & DRINKIN'

Farmers are certainly not being paid enough. The pressure has been on for years to supply cheap food at any cost. There are huge health and social issues to be considered and for farmers and horticulturalists it's disastrous. Our food should be our medicine, and yet some people think we have a God-given right to cheap food and want to pay half nothing for the food we need. *Darina Allen, founder, Ballymaloe Cookery School.*

Late *Late Late* showing

Undoubtedly I was over the limit night after night, until at some stage I was told by the director of programmes that I wasn't to drive myself home from the show any more, drunk or sober. *Road Safety Authority chairman and TV presenter Gay Byrne.*

I don't want to see anyone knocked down or injured by a drunk driver. I am not condoning drink driving, but there is no evidence that people driving below the current limit are causing accidents. The way it is going, the parish priest couldn't say two Masses as he would not be able to drink wine at the two Masses. That is just taking it too far. *Fianna Fáil TD Mattie McGrath.*

Burgermeister

The level of interest has been extraordinary. Mothers have called to say how disappointed they were that they couldn't get spice burgers any more for their kids in the local chipper; three of the multiples have been on to place orders. Well-known companies have said they're interested in the brand. *Reg Power, Walsh Family Foods, on the resumption in production of the firm's unique gastronomic creation.*

Diners right

People can be intimidated by the vast knowledge of the chef and indeed he may well have more knowledge. He is also running a business so has to accept that even when the customer is wrong they are right. *Food critic Tom Doorley.*

PARTY LINES

Deputy First Minister, I have a message for you. I am Irish as well as British. I am a Protestant and a unionist and you cannot deny me the right nor the benefits which flow from it, including a legitimate expression of my religious and cultural heritage. *Drew Nelson, Grand Orange Lodge of Ireland.*

Agin the Government
They have used a cloak of unsubstantiated claims and criticism to hide a paucity of ideas for dealing with the current crisis. They are the living, breathing, walking examples of empty vessels making the most noise. *Minister John Gormley on the Opposition.*

Sinn Féin are scundered, Fine Gael are in a lament and I have to tell the leader of the Labour Party that, contrary to his view, this Government is lean, mean and very fit . . . very fit for purpose. *Tánaiste Mary Coughlan.*

Glass distinction
If you are living on the Northside, there is no telling when you'll get approval for glasses. It's a form of health apartheid. *Cork TD Bernard Allen.*

Motion withheld
I still think they're gobshites I'm dealing with across the table. I still think they don't understand the issues. I still think they have moved very little. *Green Party TD Ciarán Cuffe on his Fianna Fáil colleagues.*

All right Jack
While we welcome the inclusion of the royal coat of arms on ID cards we are disappointed that for the sake of pandering to nationalist prejudice the Union flag will be absent upon request. This Union flag is the flag of Northern Ireland: only those who would choose to take offence because of their political bias would object to it being featured on any national identity card. *Lagan Valley MP Jeffrey Donaldson.*

Parting lines
From here on in, it's dealing with the future. We had 23 very exciting years. I think we did for our part make a fundamental difference to Irish life. We have been in government for a substantial part of our history, which we could never have anticipated in 1986 when the party was formed. *Former leader Mary Harney finally winding up the Progressive Democrats.*

MAMMON

I know we have maybe been criticised because we weren't dismal enough, but we certainly thought we were being difficult during that period. *Outgoing Central Bank governor John Hurley claims to have foreseen and forewarned of the recession.*

Dress reversal

Most areas of the business are down on last year, but the €1,000-plus suit market is the worst affected and is down 40 per cent. The €299–€599 suit market is not as badly hit, as men are trading down. The dress-down Friday look, chinos and polo shirts, is down, as men are wearing suits five days a week now as they are watching their jobs. *Exclusive menswear retailer Martin O'Byrne.*

Cutting remarks

If people used to snuff it at 70 and they've now decided to snuff it at 80, 85 or 90, then something's got to give. *Colm McCarthy, chairman, An Bord Snip Nua, on why a retirement age of 65 is now economically unacceptable.*

What Colm McCarthy has done is Dublin 4 economics. All of the people on that board are living in Dublin; there is not one of them who knows how the rural economy works. *Irish Farmers' Association leader Pádraig Walshe.*

The arts are part of this nation. Plus we employ local people; we buy local produce. There are thousands working in the arts, not all paid very well, but we do pay our taxes. We are making our case and we need to have our own minister at the cabinet table; the future of the department is being examined. As chair of the Arts Council, I'm saying this would be a retrograde step for the arts in Ireland. *Pat Moylan does not welcome the proposed cuts.*

You get this kind of feeling at times reading it that there's a bit of 'This is Ireland as viewed from the snug in Doheny and Nesbitt's' and it looks very different when you see it actually on the ground. *Labour leader Eamon Gilmore on the McCarthy report.*

If Bord na Móna had adopted McCarthy's view of life and stuck to its core activities, Bord na Móna would be out of business today. We wouldn't be capitalising on all the key skills, positional advantages and capability advantages we have developed over the years. *Managing director Gabriel D'Arcy.*

Land's end

At the height of the boom, people were buying land left, right and centre and flipping it on. It was absolutely widespread. Land would change hands but before contracts were signed and the sale was complete, it would be sold on again for a profit. A day wouldn't go by when two or three developers wouldn't come in to us mad for land. The sort of figures sound absolutely unreal now but at the time they were being bandied about every day. *Failed developer Richie Connor.*

DE MORTUIS

Frank McCourt was an author of rare ability whose vivid prose and creative ability captivated millions. However, it is his life, and not just his literary work, that will rightly be celebrated. His Pulitzer-Prize-winning masterpiece, *Angela's Ashes,* shone a light into the dark recesses of Ireland's past but it was Frank's ability to overcome such adversity that will continue to inspire thousands all around the world. *Fine Gael arts spokeswoman Olivia Mitchell. Frank McCourt died this month.*

Frank arrived in New York from Limerick with nothing and—like so many Irish immigrants before him—worked to build a better life here. He shared his gift for teaching with thousands of New York City public schoolchildren and when he retired, he shared his gift for storytelling with the world. *New York mayor Michael Bloomberg.*

The wonderful thing about Frank is that it didn't change him at all and he became a hugely beloved figure in New York, really because of his work on behalf of other writers. I think what he was best known for was just being Frank, with this incredible, low-key, deadpan humour, a wonderful supporter for young writers. Success actually improved him, which is highly unusual in this world. *Irish Voice publisher Niall O'Dowd.*

Frank did amazing things and was the greatest example of the supposedly impossible second act in life. *Writer Sebastian Barry.*

Battles long ago

She led a very full life. She loved music, and in particular opera and gardening. She helped in the local church and she had an awful lot of friends that she kept in touch with. But she never liked to speak about the sorry episode which had happened to her. *Daughter Eileen on Sheila Cloney, victim of the 1957 Fethard-on-Sea sectarian boycott. Sheila Cloney died this month.*

The Fethard-on-Sea boycott was one of the shabbiest periods in Irish history but it was also one of the most noble. It saw great moral courage by Sheila Cloney, who refused to give in to the infamous *ne temere* decree and rear a child as a Catholic. *Senator Eoghan Harris.*

LESSER BREEDS

I was getting my picture taken after the show and I looked down and I saw the snake look at me, and I knew straight away it was going to go for my face. I just closed my eyes and poked my chin forward so he wouldn't catch me in the eye. But I did get a bite in the face. Then, last January, a 6-foot lizard bit me on the neck and I had to go on antibiotics for a while, but he didn't do it maliciously. *Snake-charmer and model Emma Quinlan.*

Paper chase

The bulls went by me and I thought that was it, and that I had done well on my first run. Then this black one came by on his own. I suppose I antagonised him. I had a rolled-up newspaper and I hit him with it. *Alan Chambers, Monkstown, Co. Dublin, at the Running of the Bulls, Pamplona, Spain.*

Puck off?

This year is the thirtieth anniversary of Ireland's oldest three fairs working together: Puck Fair, the Lammas Fair in Ballycastle, Co. Antrim, and the great October Horse Fair in Ballinasloe, Co. Galway. To celebrate that, Ballycastle offered to catch a goat to become King Puck and they duly captured the king-in-waiting in Fair Head a few days ago, but when they went to get clearance to transport the king the department in the North would only give him a four-day passport. Now Ballycastle is 365 miles from Killorglin and a goat can only travel 8 hours at a time without being fed, rested and watered, and obviously we treat all our kings like royalty, so that just doesn't give us time to have him reign in Killorglin for the three-day festival. *Puck Fair chairman Declan Mangan.*

A la cart

It was just a question of picking our moment and grabbing it. It happened a fortnight ago around the time of the run-up to the Twelfth, and we felt it appropriate we call it Billy. I expect the agriculture people to give the all-clear either tomorrow or Friday and it will travel south in a goat cart. *Séamus Blaney, Moyle District Council.*

LAW & DISORDER

This unusual piece of legislation was promoted by concern within certain official circles that a tiny minority of solicitors are harvesting information on operational matters and passing them on to the criminal fraternity and effectively acting as criminal intelligence officers for criminal gangs. *Limerick state solicitor Michael Murray on the new Criminal Justice Act.*

It is wrong and dangerous that such legislation would be enacted with so much speed and so little debate. The Law Society cannot see what is driving the urgency of this. There is evidence of a problem of intimidation of witnesses but not of intimidation of juries. *Law Society Director-General Ken Murphy.*

Of course, every murder has been awful for the families of the murdered but the Roy Collins murder was different. Clearly, the murderers were sending out a signal to anyone in that community that if they assisted in any shape or form in cases against them, they would take revenge and make an example. *Minister for Justice Dermot Ahern.*

Come down here to Limerick and live my life, which I have been left with because of these thugs. Leave the leafy estates and look at what ordinary law-abiding people have to deal with. We stood up to these gangs and look what happened. *Steve Collins, father of murder victim Roy.*

FAITH & MORALS

We stood exposed, not as an island of charming saints and chatty, avuncular scholars but as a repressed, cold-hearted, fearful, smugly pious, sexually ignorant and vengeful race of self-styled Christians. *Ombudsman Emily O'Reilly on the Ryan report.*

O my God

One of the world's most beautiful and best-loved countries, Ireland has recently become one of the most respected as well: dynamic, go-ahead, modern, civilised—a green and pleasant silicone valley. This preposterous blasphemy law puts all that respect at risk. *Prof. Richard Dawkins.*

Mass appeal

Last Saturday evening you had live Saturday evening games from 3.30 p.m. until 8 p.m. You had Monaghan v Derry and Kerry v Longford in football and then Clare v Galway in hurling. That's going a bit too far when you think that those games are clashing with Saturday evening vigil Masses. *Fr Kevin McNamara, Killarney cathedral.*

No resting place

A church is not under any circumstances to serve as a funeral home. Allowing the remains to repose in a church creates talk in a place of quiet, reserve and prayer, changes a church from being a place of worship of God to a place of assembly and changes the focus from the altar and the tabernacle to an open coffin in front of the sacred space. *Fr Seán McHugh, Galway diocesan communications officer, on behalf of Bishop Martin Drennan.*

Sainted isle

We're always a worried, nervous community. Nobody knows the strength of the wind or the strength of the Atlantic waves. But, thank God, we have great belief in St Colmcille and we put our trust in Colmcille that he will protect us. *Patsaí Dan Mac Ruaidhrí, king of Toraigh.*

Cnoc on wood

People have been coming from Kerry and Clare to see this tree, which we believe shows a clear outline of Our Lady. It's doing no harm and it's bringing people together from young and old to black and white, Protestant and Catholic, to say a few prayers, so what's wrong with that? *Rathkeale, Co. Limerick shopkeeper Séamus Hogan.*

There's nothing there . . . it's just a tree. You can't worship a tree. *Local parish priest Fr Willie Russell.*

EUROPA

During that first plenary session on Tuesday I looked around and saw the 736 MEPs and I thought to myself, 'What an incredible achievement for a body set up after World War II to have all these MEPs, largely speaking, all engaged in one common purpose. We should not take that for granted. *First-time MEP Nessa Childers.*

The closest thing in my experience would be the GAA congress. The European parliament is something similar, except that you have 736 members. There's instant translation, which is great. They could do with that in the GAA congress with the different dialects; fellows from the North can't understand fellows from Kerry and vice versa. *First-time MEP and former GAA president Seán Kelly.*

Yes and no

The most memorable moment of the week was when a member of the UK Independence Party, Nigel Farage, offered his help to the Irish 'No' campaign in the Lisbon treaty referendum. This is someone who is so pro-British that he is willing to campaign hand-in-hand with Sinn Féin to make sure a treaty that enhances democracy does not get passed. It seemed quite bizarre. *First-time MEP Alan Kelly.*

A second 'No' in the forthcoming referendum, independently of any precise legal consequences, will clearly condemn us to the status of 'non-playing members'. *EU Director-General for Trade David O'Sullivan.*

It is clear that the very deregulated economic model upon which Lisbon is based is responsible for the international financial collapse. *Former Green Party MEP Patricia McKenna.*

AN t-AOS ÓG

We are very concerned about the lack of services for this age group. They are exploring their sexuality and relationships for the first time, learning their alcohol limits and what they are like as social beings outside the family. They are being targeted by sexual predators in their communities who are older, wiser and have been around the block a couple of times, who realise that they are vulnerable to being manipulated and exploited. *Fiona Neary, Rape Crisis Network.*

Uncle Ned's cabin
There is no stigma attached to being taught in a Portakabin. Many people in offices and administration across the country work in Portakabins and they are delighted to have them. I have been right in many of the things I have said in the last five to seven years, even on the economy, so I am not prepared to stand back and listen to people abusing me and telling me this, that and the other thing. *Ned O'Keeffe TD.*

I want to ask Ned O'Keeffe, how come our children go in there and they are passing out with the heat during the summer and in winter we have to put coats on our kids to keep them warm in the Portakabins? *Claire Flynn, Rathcormac, Co. Cork Parents' Association.*

Office politics
My job—and that of my office—is to speak up for children and to investigate wrongdoing. It is just inconceivable that the distinct and independent nature of my office would be tampered with, diminishing the ability of my office, with its powers and specialised skills, to speak up for the abused child, the disabled child, the child in care. *Ombudsman Emily Logan on the proposal to create a single Ombudsman Commission.*

HERE & THERE
Now, we feel like we're living in an open prison because we oppose it. We're basically under surveillance with cameras pointed at the house here, watching everything we do. I can't go down to the beach with my daughters or grandchildren. I'm no radical; we're from a big Fianna Fáil family. I'm just standing up for my family. *Shell to Sea protestor Colm Henry, Co. Mayo.*

Out of Africa
It can be really difficult to settle back after being abroad for a long time. The heightened experience in somewhere like Somalia is lost when you get home. You find yourself thinking about the way there's so much waste in the West. I'm always struck by the fact that the

average pet in Ireland has more money spent on its food that the average person in Africa's poorer regions. *Concern's Overseas Director Paul O'Brien.*

I think you know very early on if this work and a completely different lifestyle suits you or not. I mean, the living conditions can be extremely spartan. I've lived in mud huts where you might find a snake or scorpion. But once you get over the culture shock, it can be hugely rewarding. And there's something about Africa as a continent—maybe the notion that it's the cradle of civilisation—that has a remarkable pull. *Limerick doctor Simon Collins, Médecins Sans Frontières.*

Re rail

The general public might say, 'Wasn't he an awful lunatic to put that money into that train?', but this train will be there for the next 100 years. A lot of money was put into it, but it is money well spent at the end of the day, because it is part of our most important heritage in west Clare. When this was built in 1892 at a cost of £1,900 we had nothing only a donkey. *Jackie Whelan, restorer of West Clare locomotive 'Slieve Callan'.*

Metro North is some people's pet hate and they continue to feed this feeling into the media. However, the project's situation has not changed one iota. *Transport minister Noel Dempsey.*

Recycled

My wife and I were sitting out on our lawn and a servant came to tell us that a European lady had arrived on a bicycle . . . She had run out of clothes. I told her she was welcome to my wardrobe. She picked out a few pairs of trousers. She said she was not fussy and they fitted her like a glove. She was a lovely woman and she told us a lot about Ireland. *At his palace, Miangul Aurangzeb, last wadi of Swat, entertains travel writer Dervla Murphy.*

Friends in high places

Ireland is a fantastic country to fly over in a balloon, and you meet wonderful people. *Joseph Leahy, Irish Ballooning Association.*

HIS & HERS

Myself and another girl were walking along in uniform on O'Connell Street the first or second day we were out. The traffic slowed down and everything came to a standstill. At all the windows along by the Savoy and the Gresham Hotel there were people looking out. We approached a guard—how innocent we were—and we said to him, 'What's going on? Is there something happening?' He said, 'Would you go away from me, for heaven's sake. It's yourselves they're looking at.' *Former bangharda Bríd Wymbs, one of the first class of 12 of 1959.*

Fit for purpose

I heard it being discussed on the radio and they were saying men are going to be redundant. I don't think it's a good idea at all and it's not for ethical reasons or anything. Just think of all the fun you'd miss in life—men's company and courtship and love. I don't think so. *Mary O'Rourke TD.*

I like Irishmen; you always have good craic. They are dead easygoing and I love the Irish accent. When it comes to having Irishmen in bed, I'm not experienced enough to say how good they are, but I'd certainly fancy some nice Irish boys. *Porn film actress and producer Tanya Tate.*

DIY

Sex is natural but it doesn't necessarily come naturally, and there's nobody who's doing it perfectly. But, in general, there's no instructional discourse. In any sex education, whether it's formal or social, we're not given any guidance on when or how we should do what. *Psychoanalyst Ray O'Neill.*

Questions and answers

What I want to say I've already said but unfortunately it may have been very difficult for the listeners to hear because you talked over practically every single thing that I said, which you probably think is a very provocative and interesting way of doing an interview, but I don't think so at all. *Susan McKay, National Women's Council of Ireland, on 'McGurk at Four'.*

That's because I'm a man, is it? *Tom McGurk.*

It may be or it just may be that you're a particularly rude man. *Susan McKay.*

AG OBAIR
Like, personally, we find, like, we're scraping the pennies together, because, like, I have a part-time job, but now I only have work the first two weeks of every month. I'm not used to kind of, like, having to cut back, like, so it's kind of annoying. *Student Aisling Fitzpatrick, Cabinteely, Co. Dublin, like.*

Biased view
There are experts telling you how to make your bed and how to wipe a baby's arse. How did we survive before all these experts came along? I know nothing about anything and I know a tiny bit about fashion—but I know that 90 per cent of people on television who talk about fashion know nothing about it. They wouldn't know a raglan sleeve from a bias binding. *Fashion designer Peter O'Brien.*

Changing their spot
The Paddy is the best man in the world when he goes abroad to work but he's a different man at home. *Martin Sheehan, owner of waste-disposal company Mr Binman, who, he says, 'has hired non-nationals to keep manners on the Paddies'.*

PLAYING THE GAME
To hear a national coach saying, in any shape or form, gouging is acceptable in the modern-day game is despicable . . . essentially it brought the game into disrepute. *Irish rugby captain Brian O'Driscoll on South Africa coach Peter de Villiers.*

Grass routes
The turf comes from a farm in Scunthorpe . . . We looked at a number of farms around the world, including one in Slovakia which provided the pitch for the Champions League final. We were looking at the best turf for our games, studying things like ball bounce, traction, tensile strength, grass cover and on and on. These are criteria which we test on a regular basis and we were very happy with the Scunthorpe product. *Croke Park stadium director Peter McKenna on plans to relay the pitch following the U2 concerts.*

Given the history of the stadium and the pitch I think the GAA should be doing more to source sod from within Ireland rather than importing it. I'm not sure anyone involved in the GAA would be too comfortable with the notion of the All-Ireland finals being played on British soil. *Senator Mark Daly.*

The two pitches were designed with the aim of attracting Europe's leading sports teams, be it Chelsea, Liverpool, Manchester United, Barcelona . . . When they were being sown, it was done with laser technology so that the surface is absolutely flat, with one degree of gradient for drainage. To the naked eye they look completely flat. *Carton House Hotel manager David Webster prepares for the visit of Real Madrid.*

It could be the beginning of a very good relationship for the future. We are very happy because we have received a very warm welcome and the facilities and everything have been excellent. *Real Madrid technical director Emilio Butragueño.*

Jerseys milked
I'd always fancied a Down 1960 jersey, and by using archive footage from newspaper reports and old photos, I got my brother to knock me up a replica. It stimulated tremendous interest when I went to matches and friends began asking me how they could go about getting old jerseys of their own. We endeavoured to recreate a few classical GAA county jerseys of years gone by and suddenly the interest exploded. *Brian Irwin, founder, Retro GAA.*

Worth a try
The emotional impact just can't be underestimated. There are a lot of people who believe Ireland's football success in the World Cup kicked off the Celtic Tiger years. So our rugby success at the moment gives us a really important lift. Maybe it won't get us out of the gloom but I think it will stop us from sinking further. *John Trainor, Onside Sponsorship.*

Papal blessing
The other thing was that I had embraced Ireland. I love the craic. I love the people. I love Ireland and now I've lived here almost half my life . . . New Zealand is my birthright but I don't really know what I

am now. It's a tough call for me when New Zealand play Ireland. *TV rugby pundit Brent Pope.*

AND IT'S GOODNIGHT FROM HIM

We are coming to the end of simplistic dualism, of the Cartesian moment in intellectual thought. *Labour Party president Michael D. Higgins.*

It's a cut-throat business

says former RTÉ *presenter Barbara McMahon: 'It's not really a case of there being loyalty to any one person. You have to be talented and know what you are doing. If your ratings are falling, you're going to get axed, simple as that.' The axe falls, not only in the world of arts and entertainment, but now, courtesy of An Bord Snip Nua, anywhere a tall poppy is left standing. Clichés of the Year: basically; at this moment in time; 'going forward'. Closely pursued by that ubiquitous intramural pachyderm.*

Culture Ireland is the only game in town if you are an ambassador for Ireland in any country and if you are seeing that there is any way of representing our country positively in the next five years. Yeah, get Culture Ireland and send in the Druid, send in The Gate and suddenly An Bord Snip Nua says get rid of that entirely. I know what that is called. It is called knowing the price of everything and the value of nothing. *Novelist Colm Tóibín.*

Annus horribilis

The song won and what happened? Six months later I was still singing *What's Another Year* around Europe, the managers were suing each other, and I knew that I wasn't a human being any more—I was a business they were fighting over in court. They were turning up at airports, shouting at each other as I was arriving in with my suitcases. Seriously! *Johnny Logan, 1980 Eurovision winner.*

I know I am in the wrong industry for loyalty. Most people in the business are totally fake. The record companies use and abuse everybody. We think they are friends, but once things go downhill suddenly they will be in a meeting. I don't trust Americans as much as Irish people in business. *Impresario Louis Walsh.*

ARTS & PARTS

You can't understand many of the words in modern music and when you do finally work out what they're singing about, it can be embarrassing ... Many of them are about drugs, gangs and, dare I say it, sex without love ... *Singer Daniel O'Donnell.*

Landing on instruments

I was standing on the bottom rung of the dumpster and peering in. There, lying over the top, was a nasty-looking old harp. I picked it up and thought, this is interesting, although to be totally honest, I had no interest in keeping it. *New Yorker Julie Finch comes across a rare and valuable John Egan Irish harp (c. early 1800s).*

People see it as a difficult instrument, and it's certainly dominated by male players. Looking back historically, pipes were given to the male members of families, and even in terms of present-day attitudes, they're perceived to be a very difficult instrument to play. *Female piper Louise Mulcahy.*

Banned jacks

Obviously I had to get permission from the Beckett estate to stage the play in the school. I had heard that the estate was notorious for shutting down some plays so I kind of kept it on the quiet side that it was going to be set in a toilet. We got permission but it was strictly only to be seen by my classmates and the teachers in the school. No parents were allowed to come. *Harry Mitchell stages* Waiting for Godot *at his City of London school. Permission for subsequent public performance is withheld.*

Fun fare

The wonderful thing about art, it is completely and utterly useless. There's no practical value to it—that is its great joy; it is pure pleasure. *Novelist John Banville.*

Rose-tinted spectacle

I was a very normal girl, working in an office and quite shy, I suppose. Then you are thrown into this fantastic lifestyle for a year, where you are exposed to all these opportunities which you wouldn't get otherwise and meeting lots of interesting people. It was a fantastic time but life moves on. I have three kids now, school runs and all the other business. It is not something that would come into my mind every day, but this is all the more special this year because of the history. *Former Rose of Tralee Muirne Hurley (1994). The event first took place in 1959.*

I don't have a television, but that's not why I've never watched the competition. I'm just not curious about it. *First Rose Alice O'Sullivan.*

It doesn't matter what background you come from, farmer, solicitor, doctor, unemployed, your job as an escort doesn't end with those ten days in Tralee—it's only the start. No matter where you go, you have somewhere to stay and people to meet, and friends for life. *Three times Rose escort Philip Kehoe on the camaraderie between his co-participants.*

There was a countryness about it that has gone. The local involvement has more or less gone and they have brought in outsiders. The local people lost interest because they felt they weren't gaining. It's a TV event, not about the locals. The outsiders run it. *Laura Moore, Abbey Gate Hotel, Tralee.*

Igniferous rock
We did encounter a bit of resistance from people within the town. I suppose people were a little fearful of a shower of lunatics arriving on their doorsteps. But there was very little trouble and we didn't have much of a clue about how to run something that size. *Pat O'Connell, chairman of the first Macroom, Co. Cork Mountain Dew Festival 1977, the country's first open-air rock event.*

RGDATA
As a rule I always wrote about what I knew and I've never been to an orgy and wouldn't know how to describe it. *Novelist Maeve Binchy.*

CALLS OF NATURE
The allotments remind me of a time when people used to be out cutting turf on the bogs during the long evenings. They would use that time to find out all the local news. People miss that. We've gone away from that a lot and I think human nature wants that back. It's like people sort of want to get back in touch again. *Gerard McDonald, Fingal Allotments.*

Monk business
They were the first monastic order to become self-sufficient. Until then, monasteries had been dependent on receiving food as gifts from local lords. The Cistercians at Bective Abbey were far more sustainable, as they farmed 4,000 acres of land, processed their own corn and began a programme of land reclamation. *Archaeologist Dr Geraldine Stout.*

Tail-bearer
I'm obsessed with the sea. I always wanted to be a mermaid, and I guess this is the next best thing. When I finish college the aim is to work in shark conservation, which I guess is a funny one for a surfer. *Elisha Hickey, Perfect Day Surf School, Co. Sligo.*

Strictly for the birds
Really, this is aimed at the islanders, just a thank-you to them. They put up with us walking through their fields, through potato patches and sometimes into their back gardens at 6 am in the morning. And they wave at us. It's a great little community here, a great atmosphere. *Cléire bird warden Steve Wing (really), on the 50-year celebration of Cape Clear Bird Observatory.*

It is imperative that this railway embankment is put back as quickly as possible. The reason for this is that the water levels of the inner estuary at Malahide do not drain completely at low tide, creating the ideal living and feeding conditions for certain protected birds. These conditions have largely been maintained by the railway embankment, which has served in the past to restrict the water flow. In the coming weeks we will have birds arriving on Malahide estuary—they will come back expecting to find the deep water they need to dive in and they could be adversely affected by the drop in water levels. *Bird Watch Ireland development officer Niall Hatch (really).*

Under the weather
My members are telling me their customers are sick and tired of staring at rusting barbecues and soggy kids while they wait for the weather to clear up. *Jim Vaughan, Irish Travel Agents' Association, on a late surge in bookings.*

You'd be amazed how many people buy ice cream in the rain. They sit in their car and enjoy it. We also find ice cream's a really popular hangover food; you'd be amazed how busy we are on a Sunday morning. *Yasmin Khan, Teddy's, Dún Laoghaire, Co. Dublin.*

Irish people obsess just a little too much when it comes to the weather, although to some degree it is understandable given this is our third wash-out summer. *Dr Aidan Nulty, Met Éireann.*

People do not memorise what happened last summer; they regenerate it. They do not work through the summer rationally. Instead, the summer conjures up a series of images and expectations of what a really good summer is like. People are very bad at sampling data from their own memory. *Dr Michael O'Connell, UCD school of psychology.*

Traditional forecasting is based on the antics of birds, the blossoms and nature and is usually fairly accurate. For instance, if you see the heron up in the small streams and the bogs, then watch out as the rest of the month is fecked ... *Kerry traditional forecaster T.P. O'Conchuir.*

Oztensibly lethal

I can understand why he mistook it for a red-backed [sic] spider, but it's not; it's a European species. There are European spiders that can still be quite painful and unpleasant, but nothing like what you see in Australia—especially for people with sensitivity and allergy. They can kill you. *Dublin Zoo director Leo Oosterweghel is not impressed when Australian Mike Carter reports a redback find in Leixlip, Co. Kildare.*

Horse sense

The horse is a very sensitive and emotionally intelligent animal that is capable of being an effective partner in providing therapy and rehabilitation to people with mental and physical disabilities. *Kevin Smith, founder, HEALS (Horse Energy Alleviates Living Scars).*

These horses are the innocent victims of the Celtic Tiger years, when everyone owned the leg of a racehorse and there was plenty of money to care for them. Horses are rotting to a slow and painful death in fields around our country and this situation is set to deteriorate as the weather gets colder and the grass on which most of them are currently surviving disappears. *Jimmy Cahill, DSPCA (Dublin Society for the Prevention of Cruelty to Animals).*

Her feet is sealed
He came and took my foot in his mouth. I could feel his teeth. I lay still but he still came at me. He clawed my back and leg. He kept trying to grab my feet. He was a big bull and I could feel his whiskers on my toes, he went right underneath me and scratched my back. He kept coming back and I thought, 'Holy God, what part of me is he going to grab this time?' *Breda Kenny receives the close attentions of a seal at Sandycove's Forty Foot.*

STATE OF THE NATION
I think the rise of sectional interest groups who will become more willing to engage in civil unrest and protest marches and demonstrations will grow. It could be that we are not the mature democratic civil society that we might like to think we are. It may well be that Irish civil society is a thin shell that has no strong political yolk to sustain it. *UCD sociologist Tom Inglis.*

Ireland expectorates
We have seen the harbingers of civil unrest with the protests but I don't ultimately know how things will pan out. Irish people are noted for their courtesy and gentleness and they don't act like French farmers. They would have traditionally shown respect for the employees of institutions, so spitting at bank staff and verbally abusing them is a new and worrying departure. *Psychiatrist Patricia Casey.*

Just deserts
People had enough of military activity in this area during the Troubles. They thought a decent night's sleep would be part of the peace dividend. They don't want low-flying helicopters nor anything to do with a war which they don't support. British military spokesmen tell us now important this training is for operations in Afghanistan. There are very few Arabs and no sand in Ardboe. We have no connection with this war and no interest in being connected to it. *SDLP Assembly member Patsy McGlone, Co. Tyrone.*

Young Irelanders

We displayed the usual ambivalence of adolescence: grandiosity countered by sporadic deep insecurity, egocentricity countered by bouts of idealism, struggling for autonomy countered by over-dependence on others to solve our problems, living for now without too much thought for the future. We went on a gigantic spending spree. We rejected the overtures of the cousins in Europe and thought we did not need them and their strange ways any more. *Psychologist Maureen Gaffney.*

Scots free

What has the Irish Government done since the Good Friday agreement to protect human rights for Protestants in the Republic? Where is the quota recruitment for the Garda, where is the Policing Board for the Garda, where is parity of esteem for Ulster Scots 11 years after the Agreement? Nothing has changed. Catch yourselves on and tidy up your own act first. *Ulster Unionist Lord John Laird.*

SICKNESS & HEALTH

After relentless lobbying by myself and the people of the north-west, I was unable to influence Minister Harney of the justifiable case of the retention of the cancer services in Sligo General Hospital, and I have been left with no alternative but to resign the whip. *Sligo North Leitrim TD Eamon Scanlon.*

This is not about Jimmy Devins or about Fianna Fáil. This is about patients' lives. *Sligo North Leitrim TD Jimmy Devins resigns the whip.*

Many take the view that it is nothing other than a choreographed charade to mislead the public into thinking they are taking an action that is in the interests of the hospital and the people in the region when, in fact, it is merely about their own political survival. *Sligo cancer services campaigner Jim O'Sullivan.*

How can they let this happen? If dogs on the street were treated in this way, the RSPCA would be on the backs of this Government. This is inhumanity at its worst. To make people in pain travel up to 350 miles for treatment away from their family and friends is nothing short of cruelty, especially when we have an excellent service in Sligo. *Ann McGowan, Ballyshannon, Co. Donegal.*

Innpatient exit

He came into the bar, I was in the office at the time, and the girl behind the bar came in to me and said, 'There's a guy here with his robe on and drips in both his hands and he doesn't look very well.' He had asked for a drink and we refused on the basis that he had obviously walked out of the hospital. Then he took a soft drink. We read his name off his armband and phoned the Ulster Hospital and after a wee while they worked out he had come over from the hospital and one of our guys just took him back over again. *Stephen McMillan, Old Moat Inn, Belfast.*

SOCIAL & PERSONAL

When she travelled abroad as President, she would place a light in her window that would draw people of Irish descent to pass by below. Today, as an advocate for the hungry and the hunted, the forgotten and the ignored, Mary Robinson has not only shone a light on human suffering, but illuminated a better future for our world. *President Obama, awarding Mrs Robinson the Presidential Medal of Freedom.*

If you are a human rights person, you have to be fair, you have to be unbiased when you're addressing situations of human rights violations. That's the pledge of my life and that's what I live by. *Mary Robinson, responding to criticism by us pro-Israel groups.*

Cop on

People always had great peace of mind when a garda was living in a village. He knew his community well, people could approach him easily and his presence also acted as a deterrent to crime. But gardaí are losing touch with the people. If what little policing is left in rural areas is now withdrawn, people, especially the elderly in isolated districts, will be left totally exposed to highly mobile criminals who will gladly avail of all the opportunities for crime that fall into their laps. *Kerry mayor Bobby O'Connell.*

Order of the bath

In our day the only en-suite was a chamber pot. And we must have stunk to high heaven, because we were only allowed into the bath when someone else got out. There would be scum on the surface of the water, if you lay still for more than two minutes. *Musician Charlie McGettigan.*

Flour power

A wagon of turf from Shragh, where we came from, was £5 and that £5 would buy you 10 stone of flour, which was talked about as a half-sack of flour. You'd make 140 griddle cakes out of that. It would do a good household with six or seven in the family for two months. And then, when you had the flour out of the bag you'd have a sheet made for the bed out of the bag or two pillow cases. *West Clare Railway restorer Jackie Whelan.*

Decline and fall

I'm very fortunate to be an amoral person, at least when it comes to judging other people. In terms of sex, religion, politics, gambling and all forms of moral things, I am on the lowest ground. It's quite funny really—when I was in politics a lot of people, because of my Protestant background, would be saying, 'Tut, tut, Ivan, how could you get into such a lowlife occupation?' And then when I was leaving politics to go into bookmaking, all the politicians said to me, 'That really is the lowest form of animal life—dealing with gambling and so on.' Now that I've moved into the media, arguably I've gone even further downhill in some people's eyes. *Former cabinet minister Ivan Yates.*

Your only man

I'm the world's most unusual tour guide. How wonderful is this to have the continuity now of the eighth generation to be involved in this site? *St James's Gate guide Rory Guinness, son of the last family chairman of Arthur Guinness, Son & Co. Ltd.*

When I was young I'd stick my finger in someone's pint and think it tasted disgusting. I hated it for years and years. I wouldn't drink anything else now. I'd never go into a pub and drink wine. I'd feel silly. And Guinness is good for you. *Jasmine Guinness.*

HIS & HERS

I am only the Lord Mayor's wife and I am doing my duty. *Left-leaning Joe Costello TD arrives in traditional style at the Dublin Horse Show with Lord Mayor Emer.*

Arms and the man

When I first started dating him, I was like, 'Oh my God! The size of his arms.' There are certain advantages having a boyfriend called Bod. *Amy Huberman on fiancé Brian O'Driscoll.*

Limerick leader

I was surprised to be on it. I was surprised to be up there in such august company with all the handsome fellas around town. I don't know what it is. It is nothing immediately obvious to me, anyway. *Minister Willie O'Dea on being voted one of Limerick's sexiest men.*

Bag and baggage

Oh, yes, I've had some man bags. Men are quite selfish with their bags. You won't find dummies for their sons or daughters or chew bars for their dogs. Everything they carry is about them. *Handbag analyst Debbie Percy at Dublin's Ultimate Girls' Day.*

Popular friction

Her breasts are a different colour to the rest of her. It's because of all the rubbing they get from the lads—a bit like touching St Peter's foot in the Vatican. *David Denham, Dublin City Business Improvement District, on the Molly Malone sculpture.*

ROUND THE WORLD FOR SPORT

This is a dream come true, not only for me, but for boxers throughout the world who have worked so hard to gain Olympic status. *Irish champion Katy Taylor on the announcement that female boxing will feature in the 2012 games.*

Stroke play

You have to stroke the squad like a cat. You have to be gentle. The squad have got the results so far—and in this instance, you have to treat the squad like a cat. If you rub a cat in the right place it will purr and everything will be all right. But if not ... *Republic of Ireland manager Giovanni Trapattoni.*

The cruel sea

We didn't keep radio watch. We were racing, don't forget, and it was hard going. The 30-foot-high seas meant you could stay on the helm for only 20 minutes at a time. Our one meal in 24 hours was a few tins of spaghetti. I've never told the crew this, but some of the spaghetti spilled on to sails lying on the deck and I had to scrape it off and put it back in the tin before handing it round with just one spoon for 11 people. We finished the course, though survival was more important than the race. *Kevin Lane, former admiral, Royal Cork Yacht Club, recalls the disastrous 1979 Fastnet race.*

We capsized twice, bent our mast, two people went overboard but were wearing harnesses and were recovered. The first we knew of the scale of the disaster was when an RAF Sea King helicopter pilot hovering over us told us on the VHF radio that he couldn't do anything for us as he had to pick up a body. We were shocked to hear that anybody had been lost. I haven't talked about it much since. *Kevin Burke, crew on* Rapparee.

Hooping it up
All my friends think I'm crazy to play croquet, but when I tell them you can drink and smoke at the same time they get the picture. *Su Stenhouse, Glasgow, at the Croquet Championship of Ireland.*

Holding fourth
Honestly, I was just gutted out there, looking up at the clock and seeing I got fourth. I was trying not to have a little cry, because I say it all the time, I just love winning bloody medals. I love standing on podiums. And fourth is always a hard place to be. *Derval O'Rourke after her placing in the 400m hurdles at the Berlin World Championships.*

Keane edge
Some of the players here have lost their way. Some of them have fallen into the comfort zone. This is Ipswich. Guys come here on a decent wage, to a nice area with nice people, and they just coast. They won't be coasting with me; they know that. *Manager Roy Keane.*

Insect play
I think the big factor was that we seemed to be like startled earwigs in the first 15 minutes. *Dublin football manager Pat Gilroy on the team's heavy defeat by Kerry.*

Unforgiving minutes
The combination of two of the worst aspects of Irish society, short bursts of violence, punctuated by committee meetings. *Senior GAA figure Jarlath Burns takes a tongue-in-cheek view of the national games.*

CÓRAS IOMPAIR
These services are vital to people residing in rural areas, and they provide services for the elderly and for many people who reside on their own or in isolated areas, and fulfil an important social need of enabling these people to attend hospital appointments, or conduct private business, or even attend certain events. *Willie Penrose TD on the threat to the Rural Transport Scheme.*

Ryanire
It's a nightmare. Ryanair have abdicated responsibility. They have not spoken to any of these people, there have not been any public announcements and they have not said when the flights are called. The police are here with machine guns, supposed to be protecting us from terrorists, but they end up protecting Ryanair ticket sellers. It's absurd. *The BBC's David Dimbleby gets stuck in Stansted.*

Noel Dempsey and the Department of Transport are the useless shits that are overseeing the protection of the airport monopoly. In trying to protect the airport monopoly and Aer Lingus's position, they have actually done more to destroy it, and it will be broke within two years. *Ryanair CEO Michael O'Leary.*

No-go areas
I think that's absolutely pernicious, allowing people travel to places they don't want to go to, where they will not be happy. That kind of travel is bad for people. It narrows the mind. *Novelist John Banville disapproves of budget airlines.*

FAITH & MORALS
I would see that, for example, [in the case of] people in second unions and the idea of permanently excluding them for reception of the sacraments. I find that very difficult. Again, there is the whole question—I find it difficult to understand why women are excluded from full participation in ministry. I find these things difficult to

understand. With any teaching we have to try and understand the reasons behind it. *Retiring Bishop of Killaloe Willie Walsh on personal dilemmas.*

Muffled report

I'm ashamed by the Church's response to the Ryan report. It has been more about improving the Church's image than tackling fundamental problems. In the 1970s, I was sent around schools to recruit pupils to the priesthood. I couldn't do that now. *Fr Aidan Troy, latterly of Ardoyne, Belfast.*

Mosqueteer

I was born and brought up in Limerick. My kids, they're brought up in Ireland, and I don't think I'm going to move anywhere else; my soil is here. So I think it's mine and my family's duty, with the Muslim community in Ireland, who accompany many non-Muslims, who don't understand Islam, to show them the respect, to invite them. *Mia-Manan Hameed, whose father set up the Anwar e-Madina mosque in Dublin's Talbot Street.*

Pilgrims' egress

There's a certain euphoria around but it's more than that. There's hope, there's enthusiasm, there's energy, there's a kind of cleansing as well; it's a whole bodily feeling. People feel spiritually and mentally refreshed as well as bodily refreshed, even though the body is tired. I would suggest that there's a detoxification aspect to this and that's part of the good feeling. *Monsignor Richard Mohan, Lough Derg pilgrimage centre.*

The hardest thing is the shoes. You miss the shoes. If you didn't have to do without the shoes it would be easier. When you get around St Brigid's Cross a few times without the shoes, you know you're flying it. *Clare pilgrim Michael Hunt at Lough Derg.*

What's in a name

Derry needs babies called Columba. When a society honours its founder, it associates itself with the values and charisms of that person. In honouring Columba, our city will flourish. For example, when parents are honoured in their home, the family is enabled to progress. Likewise, the devotion to Colmcille will be for the well-being of Derry and it will benefit the city in every way to invoke its patron's help. *Fr Roland Colhoun, Long Tower parish.*

Hell hath no fury

What, if any, role can religion, taken in the broadest sense of that word, have in a future Ireland? The values vacuum that has replaced the authoritarianism of the past is quite alarming. The dungeon, fire and sword that had kept the faith of our fathers alive have been replaced by foreign holiday villas, suvs and Sunday mornings at Aldi. *Emeritus professor of theology Seán Freyne.*

BRICKS & MORTAR

We didn't expect to find the walls of the original three theatres but through this scraping away we unearthed the three lives of the theatres. It's a great day for the country and the world history of the theatre. *Smock Alley Theatre director Patrick Sutton on the discoveries on the site of the 1662, 1700 and 1735 Dublin theatres in the course of reconstruction.*

Brewing trouble

Heineken treated us extremely well and they were very nice and I was very impressed with the restoration work they had done on Murphy's brewery, so I just fail to understand why they will not do the same thing on the Beamish and Crawford site. I hope there will be a change of mind. *Damien Cassidy, National Conservation & Heritage Group.*

Hallmark

We've a kind of living history here, so to speak. My family is synonymous with the place, and once that goes, you lose a sense of your identity. I can trace my family very accurately as far back as 1510 and less accurately for another 150 years before that. *Thomas Cosby of Stradbally Hall, host to Electric Picnic.*

Bridge over troubled waters

The first inkling I had that something was wrong was when I noticed water splashing up to a high level. In that location, it's not a normal thing to happen, so I looked at the northbound line and saw that the track was hanging. Immediately then I could feel the ballast moving on the line beneath my train and realised the danger we were in. It was such an unreal sight. I started thinking to myself, 'Did I really see that?' *Driver Keith Farrelly, crossing the Broadmeadow, Co. Dublin estuary just before the collapse of the viaduct.*

Both tracks are gone. There are cables sticking out of the bridge and two of the arches have fallen into the water ... There were people sailing on sailboards who didn't even notice. *Malahide resident Joan McAllister.*

The scale of the potential disaster was enormous. The fact that nobody was hurt and there wasn't a derailment doesn't take away from the fact that this was very close to being a very serious tragedy. *Barry Kenny, Iarnród Éireann.*

Monumental disgrace

The statue was first put up a few years ago and was repeatedly vandalised by self-proclaimed neo-Nazis, left-wingers, right-wingers and history revisionists. Then sovereignty groups went to the memorial after the vandalism and cleaned it with yellow paint, which is not really fixing it at all. We're asking all groups, whether vandals or cleaners, to please leave the grave alone. *Seán Whelan, National Graves Association, on the statue of Seán Russell in Fairview Park, Dublin.*

Borderline case

You couldn't make it up. What about all those pleadings from the Ministers to the people to demonstrate their patriotism and shop locally instead of seeking bargains across the Border? You would think they might like to practise what they preach. Does anybody think for one minute that if a construction job had to be done at an army barracks in the North it would go to a company south of the Border? *Ballyshannon mayor Eugene Dolan objects to a €1.5m building contract for Finner Camp going to Omagh, Co. Tyrone.*

THE LONG GOODBYE

Bismarck set the retirement age at 65; it was in the late 1870s. If you work out the actuarial data and apply it to today, retirement should be at 75 or 80. *DCU President Ferdinand von Prondzynski.*

Index